EMPOWERING LEADERS

TOOLS TO CHANGE CHURCH CULTURE

"Andy and Ted have written a very practical book for pastors and laity striving for new purpose and ministry in the post-pandemic world. They are correct, it's all about culture. Culture overrides everything! Learning how to become culture creators and crafters can help your congregation find its vitality and become authentic, kingdom empowering movements. Their understanding of the steps of transformational leadership will be very beneficial to a church's leadership team. I highly recommend this book."

— Bishop Bob Farr, Missouri Annual Conference of The United Methodist Church

"Andy and Ted model something which is frequently missing: true cooperative leadership between laity and clergy. All too often, laity and clergy speak past each other, failing to understand particular contexts and needs. Even worse, misunderstanding may devolve into blaming: 'If only our pastor had better skills,' or 'If only the laity would become more committed.' Neither is helpful. Instead, Ted and Andy offer a way forward here. Their model for partnering in order to change congregational culture is both comprehensive and very practical. As you follow the model, we believe, that you will see positive growth and change even as so many congregations have already experienced. You will find *Empowering Leaders: Tools to Change Church Culture* to be a significant asset in your faithful ministry together."

— Janet and Philip Jamieson

"Post-pandemic challenges accelerated the need for change and in turn intensified the stresses placed on church leaders--especially the pastor. However, preaching about change has fallen flat. A commendable option: pastors learning to partner with church leaders to implement sustainable changes. Good news! These two--a vocational pastor and a seasoned layman, walk pastors and their leaders through the necessary interactions and behaviors needed--FROM BOTH SIDES OF THE AISLE. Essential reading!"

— Jim Griffith, Griffith Coaching

"Church leadership is different. It just is. It requires the clear why of scripture and conviction. It depends on communal collaboration and suffers under lone rangers, no matter how good. It is specific to place which requires a clear diagnostic eye. And, it is forever changing. For leaders willing to take it on, Andy and Ted have provided resources, tools, experience, and reflections - not to be read through once - but to be visited often. Thank you Andy and Ted."

— Gil Rendle, Consultant, teacher and author of multiple books on church leadership including *Countercultural: Subversive Resistance and the Neighborhood Congregation*

We dedicate this book to the Christian servants and leaders in the congregations we served and to the scholars of Mid-Atlantic United Methodist Foundation stewardship programs. You have partnered with us and inspired us.

EMPOWERING LEADERS

TOOLS TO CHANGE CHURCH CULTURE

ANDY LUNT & TED BROWN

Empowering Leaders: Tools to Change Church Culture
Copyright © 2023 by Andy Lunt & Ted Brown
Published by Lucid Books in Houston, TX
www.LucidBooks.com

All rights reserved. No part of this publication may be reproduced, stored in a retrieval system, or transmitted in any form by any means, electronic, mechanical, photocopy, recording, or otherwise, without the prior permission of the publisher, except as provided for by USA copyright law.

Unless otherwise noted Scripture quotations are taken from the Holy Bible, New International Version®, NIV®. Copyright ©1973, 1978, 1984, 2011 by Biblica, Inc.™ Used by permission of Zondervan. All rights reserved worldwide. www.zondervan.com The "NIV" and "New International Version" are trademarks registered in the United States Patent and Trademark Office by Biblica, Inc.™

Scripture quotations marked (MSG) are taken from THE MESSAGE, copyright © 1993, 2002, 2018 by Eugene H. Peterson. Used by permission of NavPress. All rights reserved. Represented by Tyndale House Publishers, Inc.

Anselm Companion to the Bible: With NSRV Translation. Winona, MN: Anselm Academic, 2014.

ISBN: 978-1-63296-598-1
eISBN: 978-1-63296-599-8

TABLE OF CONTENTS

Forward i

Introduction And Executive Summary 1

Empowering Laity For Ministry 13
    Tools 41

Focusing on Purpose and Identity 75
    Tools 85

Discerning Culture 95
    Tools 105

Shifting Culture 111
    Tools 127

Leading - A Shared Responsibility 155
    Tools 171

Dealing with People 183
    Tools 193

Overcoming Resistance and Barriers 199
    Tools 207

Caring for Leaders 221
    Tools 229

Envisioning a Changed Culture 233

APPENDIX
    A. Benefits of Coaching 243
    B. One Church's Transformation Story 247

Acknowledgments 254

FORWARD

Church leaders are searching for ways to address a situation unlike what they have experienced in their lifetimes. After a relatively stable decade in the 1990s, a major downward trend in attendance began in 2002 and continues today. The pandemic cannot be blamed for all of today's challenges. As disruptive as it was, it merely exacerbated and accelerated trends underway for years and even decades. For example, even as church statistics appeared stable in the 1990s, a new phenomenon was emerging. It was in these years that the number of "nones" began to increase dramatically. Nones are those who claim no religious affiliation. The vast majority of the new nones came from the younger generations. Since the young participate less in church life, their presence was not immediately noticeable in congregations. However, these nones have not followed the pattern of previous generations in becoming more religiously active as they grow older. Therefore, the higher number of nones grows even larger. When this change is combined with the increasing age of church members, increasing costs of operation with fewer donors, and the deaths and disruption from the pandemic, no wonder church leaders feel ill-equipped for what they face today.

Andy Lunt and Ted Brown offer a rich resource for congregations and their leaders to engage today's circumstances with confidence and hope. They build their work around three essential components of any lasting change.

Purpose and Identity

The church begins every chapter of its life remembering that we build on a solid rock that is God's purpose for the Church and for our congregation. You've heard of being "between a rock and a hard place." Let's think, rather, of our church situation today as "between a solid rock and a new place." Remember the words from Isaiah 51:1, "Look to the rock from which you were hewn, and to the quarry from which you were dug." It may seem counterintuitive to focus on mission, identity, and history if the goal is to do something new to meet a changed context. Quite the opposite is the case. It is only through becoming clear about who you are, what you have been, and the calling God has for your church that you can begin to shape the future. Your mission and history are your foundation. It is your congregational DNA. Your church may change, but it will carry much of its DNA with it.

So why is it we need anything other than our solid rock? The Bible also says, "Where there is no vision, the people perish" (Proverbs 29:18). Theologically, we know that the way things are now – whether in our lives or in our congregation – is never synonymous with God's ultimate will. We cannot become what God needs for us to be by remaining what we are. So we begin with our foundation of mission and identity. We assess our situation. Then through prayer and spiritual discernment, we identify that new thing Isaiah writes that God has for us: "I am about to do a new thing: do you not perceive it?" (43:19)

Partnership with Laity

All leaders do well to remember Paul's analogy for the church in I Corinthians 12: It is the body with its multiple and different parts that is of greatest importance. Much conventional wisdom about leadership assumes a leader working alone, but the solo leader is rarely associated with effective leadership. The best leaders build teams. Collaboration acknowledges in a dramatic way our mutual need for and appreciation of one another.

Living into a new vision, the new thing God has for us, is about change; therefore, collaboration with others is essential for a healthy and fruitful transition. Change within organizations is never as simple and one-dimensional as it may seem to the leader seeking to be a change agent.

Power is not a fixed sum in which if one person has more, another must have less. A better understanding is of power as an expandable sum where leaders and constituents are willing to be mutually influenced by one another. The more influence a leader entrusts to others, the more others are willing to grant influence to the leader. The concern of good leaders is not with who receives credit for success. Their fulfillment comes in the realization of the vision to which God is calling the whole body.

Congregational Culture

Leaders of churches need to remember that congregations have personalities and cultures just as all organizations do. A church's culture encompasses its deeply held values and unwritten norms. It is so embedded into daily life that it is taken for granted. Culture shapes such things as the role of clergy and laity, how decisions are made, openness to change, acceptance of newcomers, among other things. There is no way to understand the dynamics of a congregation without knowing its culture. While the overt expressions of the culture can be observed, deeper analysis is required to understand their mental and emotional underpinnings.

The culture of an organization provides the most important lever for genuine and long-term change. Any change that does not engage the heart of a culture is superficial at best and will not last long. It is not enough for leaders to know "what needs to be done." Effective leaders also understand the cultural context in which change takes place. Change and culture work in tandem. If brilliant strategy does not have a healthy culture to carry it, the strategy will not work. No matter what is said by a leader or even approved by a board, little will change unless the direction is reinforced within the cultural fabric of the congregation.

Next Step is Yours

Lunt and Brown bring distinctive and varied experience and perspectives to their writing. You will benefit from their wisdom and practical guidance. They believe in the church as God's instrument in the world for redemption and grace. They also believe in the ability of ordinary leaders to do extraordinary things through a dedicated group of laity and the power of God. Remember that all of you are leaders, and that leaders help God's people take their next faithful step.

Lovett H. Weems, Jr., is a distinguished professor of church leadership emeritus at Wesley Theological Seminary in Washington, DC, and the author of many books on church leadership. His latest (with F. Douglas Powe, Jr.) is *Sustaining While Disrupting: The Challenge of Congregational Innovation* (Fortress Press, 2022)

CHAPTER 1
INTRODUCTION AND EXECUTIVE SUMMARY

The congregation was radically divided into two opposing camps. One strongly supported the pastor and talked down any who opposed him. Others did everything they could to discredit and sabotage any initiatives supported by the pastor.

A consultant was called in to observe and make recommendations. After a series of meetings with many in the congregation, both individually and in small groups, it became apparent that the pastor should be removed. The environment had become so toxic that a drastic action was necessary, even though it could be interpreted as a win for the anti-pastor faction.

The consultant then created a task force including leaders from both opposing camps. It eventually became clear that the majority of the congregation had not taken sides and actually wanted the divisiveness to end.

At an emotional meeting of the task force, the consultant confronted the group with a challenge. "Unless you are willing to stand in front of the congregation and publicly commit to stop the backbiting and demonization of one another, I see no possibility for a healthy future."

After a time of prayerful discernment, the task force members indicated their willingness, and a Sunday was set for the declaration. The consultant preached on the nature of the church and then introduced the members of the task force who stood in front of the congregation and committed themselves to work together with a renewed focus on the purpose of the church. The consultant, then extended an invitation for any others to come forward and join in the same commitment. All but five of the 200 in attendance came forward. Several years and two pastors later, the congregation is growing and thriving.

This is just one example of how a toxic culture can hinder a congregation's ministry, what can happen when pastors and laity do not lead together, and how a renewed commitment to a shared purpose can lead to transformation and renewal.

Churches everywhere are struggling and in need of such transformation. We live in a time of unprecedented change. COVID, racial discord, rising crime, and bitter divisiveness in both church and society present all churches with the challenge of finding a faithful way forward in the midst of chaos and change.

Although experts from many disciplines have written and spoken about a "new normal," in reality there is no such thing as "normal". Normal has always been and, even more so now, is highly contextual. What is normal in one community would be seen as an aberration in another.

Without question the environment for Christian congregations has changed and is continuing to change. Established precedent and procedures are being questioned and frequently discarded for the newest best practice. All this change has led to a climate of widespread fear and anxiety.

In this environment of change, the process of seeking answers has caused suspicion, bitterness and open hostility within communities, denominations, and individual congregations. Instead of experiencing cooperation and compromise, we witness competition that seeks winners and losers (or right and wrong), and a scenario that hardly resembles the "body of Christ."

Our work with congregations has led us to understand that the best way to move forward into a new and ever-changing world is to focus on (1) purpose and identity, both individually and as a faith community, (2) new ways of partnering between clergy and laity and (3) a deeper understanding of the role of culture (behavior based on deep-rooted values and unwritten social norms) in effecting lasting change.

In this difficult and chaotic time of change we invite you to ponder these questions:

- Are most of your church members thriving and growing in commitment and discipleship? Or are they worn out and drained by the last few years, or have perhaps even fallen away?
- Are your ministries vibrant? Or are they on a plateau or perhaps even in decline?
- Are you leading transformation and finding meaning and excitement in your ministries? Or has nothing changed, despite your best efforts to employ the latest techniques?
- Do you have a clear sense of the path toward a compelling future for your faith community? Or are you caught in a time of change with no idea what to do?
- If you are a pastor, are you feeling overwhelmed and exhausted? If you are a layperson, do you feel powerless to make a difference? Are you burned out? Is the world challenging you or are you challenging it?
- Is your leadership fulfilling or frustrating for you? What would need to change to make it more rewarding and productive?
- Do you and other leaders have a clear sense of your purpose as individuals and as a congregation?

If these questions spark your desire to re-energize your church's ministries, your members' vitality, and your own sense of purpose and excitement, this book is for you. We will provide a framework with methods and tools to (1) empower laity, who live as kingdom dwellers, to grow into kingdom builders; (2) inspire laity and pastors to lead as partners in ministry; (3) challenge leaders to create a church purpose and identity that excites and motivates others to follow; and (4) cultivate an environment of generosity among all laity that provides abundant resources for mission and ministry.

The uniqueness of this book comes from blending two independent experiences and observations – one a lay perspective and the other a pastor's perspective. While these experiences and observations occurred in one denomination, conversations with leaders in several other denominations revealed similar observations. This book promotes aligned pastor and laity perspectives on laity empowerment, leadership, analysis of culture and the means to shift it, ramifications of change for all leaders, and a healthy response to resistance and barriers. The framework, methods, and tools cited here have been adapted from leadership and culture change in the secular world and successfully used in churches.

Through more than 40 years as a pastor and director of congregational development, co-author Andy Lunt became aware of the importance of culture shift in churches. His experience and work with dozens of churches sharpened his understanding of a necessary shift. He saw the need for clergy and laity to partner together for vital ministry coupled with the hard work of changing culture. Andy realized this most fully when he was called in to consult with a church where people were working hard to advance ministry but getting nowhere. The relatively new pastor was putting in long hours but failed to delegate when necessary. He was feeling the weight of leadership and the sense that everything depended on him and his efforts. He was exhausted, his family suffered, and little was changing. On the other hand, many gifted laypersons were working equally hard in various ministries, many of which had long existed but were losing steam. Unfortunately, their efforts frequently conflicted with those of other ministries, resulting in competition for apparently scarce resources.

In this case two major problems were revealed. First, there was no common purpose toward which all the effort was directed. Each group was pursuing their own sense of purpose for their area of ministry. They resembled a football team with individual players running about without advancing the ball to the goal line. Secondly, the pastor and lay leaders were engaged in silo leadership rather than partnering together to lead. This is a situation found in many congregations of all sizes and cultures.

Through more than 60 years as a church member and 30 years in leadership, co-author Ted Brown recognized three important factors: (1) pastors must be more multi-dimensional in their leadership skills than any CEO he has worked with, (2) enormous parallels exist between leadership in business and in the church, and 3) laity need to be stakeholders in their church and in its purpose and identity. One story illustrates Ted's experience.

A church grew substantially over twenty-five years as their only pastor developed and empowered laity. Many ministries thrived inside and outside the church. When that pastor was replaced by a minister who preferred to command and control, the empowered laity leadership left. The new laity leadership, who were kingdom dwellers, grew frustrated with not one but two replacement pastors. They cited the lack of progress without understanding that the culture had changed. Ted was called in to consult with church leadership at this point. Although Ted provided many methods and tools to repurpose this church and identify crucial paradigm shifts, the culture of the remaining laity did not allow them to be kingdom builders (leaders).

Andy and Ted first met as leaders in the Financial Leadership Academy sponsored by the Mid Atlantic United Methodist Foundation. Andy served as dean and Ted was one of the coaches. While Ted and Andy grew up in the culture of white mainline churches, their more recent work has taken them into multiple cultures. Andy's work in congregational development in the Maryland and Washington D.C. area involved congregations that were more than 40 percent African American. Many of the materials in this book were used in Session 3 of the Financial Leadership Academy after the leadership and culture change void was noted in sessions 1 and 2. The feedback from the 95 students (30 percent African-American, 4 percent Asian, 3 percent Hispanic and 63 percent White) in Session 3 showed the broad applicability of our approach to various cultures.

Most pastors and lay leaders in all churches want to improve their church vitality and motivate their congregation to "go and make disciples of all nations, baptizing them in the name of the Father and of the Son and of the Holy Spirit". Despite the increasing secularization of society and the substitution of personal rights for the common good, this goal has not changed. In the past we have thought great preaching, better buildings, and excellent programs would encourage people to walk into our churches, where we could assimilate them into our faith community. But like everything else, the mission field of our local community, has changed. People used to attend church because it was a societal norm, the expectation in social and business circles. But, through time, the perceived value of church has faded, and people chose other activities for their time and resources. Recent events are also exposing divisions within our faith communities. These divisions vary from church to church and include deeply held beliefs about race, public policy, political platforms, and more.

Many church consultants and books focus on doing, such as improving practices and procedures. By contrast, our experience suggests that these traditional change approaches often fail to produce sustained, desired results. Most often, this is because they occur without changing the mindsets about the nature and purpose of the church. They occur in a culture that is not conducive to change. As a result, we have observed the root cause of the dilemma facing many churches is in their being—their culture, rather than their doing—their practices. We address the being by assessing the current culture and then working with leadership to move from the current condition to one that more fully reflects God's will for the local church and each individual.

The intended audience of this book are the pastors of local churches and denominational leaders who coach and guide those pastors. Occasionally, an enlightened lay leader will drive this effort, but in most cases it is the pastor who initiates the change and provides the momentum. We are aware that the key concepts we advocate—lay empowerment and leading culture change—are not usually part of seminary curricula. We hope that our work might lead to their inclusion. It is our desire that each pastor who is inspired by this book engages laity leadership in a partnership through these pages. The aim of this partnership is the desired culture shift that produces God's will for the local church.

The change in culture and personal leadership that we advocate is NOT EASY. We provide the **Stages of Transformational Leadership** as a guide:

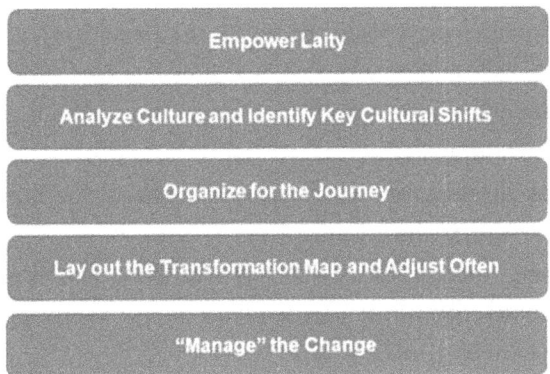

For some churches, the change will be so counter-cultural that the misunderstanding and reluctance to change will be analogous to the response that Jesus encountered as he, too, advocated counter-cultural thinking and behavior. Again, this is not easy but addressing the root cause of malaise and division never is.

Although the change in individual practices within the framework shown above is relatively easy, congregations married to the past will find even those changes challenging.

We recommend a coach (consultant) in change management, particularly church change management, to help the church move forward. A coach serves as a sounding board, mirror, and tool provider as you (laity and pastor) lead your congregation to the calling God has for your church. (A more detailed discussion of the nature and value of coaching can be found in Appendix A.) The following pages provide the means to analyze and change the culture of your church, bringing it closer to God's calling for your local faith community.

WHAT TO EXPECT

This book is a practical guide of frameworks, methods, and tools that create a recipe for cultural change. Every pastor is unique and every congregation is unique. Their transformation plans, like regional recipes, will reflect cultural differences. Regional recipes reflect local ingredients, substitutions that add unique flavors, open fire versus oven cooking, and the cook's experience. You can study a cookbook all you want but the real learning occurs during the preparation and cooking. Likewise, we have found that it is easier to "act your way into a new process of thinking" than to "think your way into a new process of acting". While the doing can be described in books, seminars and software apps, being is best understood as a path of discovery.

There are three primary and essential ingredients in the recipe for changing congregational culture. The first, and in many cases most difficult, ingredient is to embrace and implement the empowering and equipping of laity for ministry. Clergy and laity working together as partners is vital before adding the next two components. When either clergy or laity try to "do it alone" the result is usually competition, hurt feelings, and little discernible change.

The second ingredient in the change recipe is a renewed focus on purpose and identity. These become a uniting force and drive every decision and action. With laity empowered and a clear sense of purpose and identity it then becomes possible to engage the hard work of discerning and changing culture – the third ingredient. We will deal in depth with each of these ingredients in the next three chapters.

The first ingredient is empowerment – setting expectations and freeing laity for ministry.

In **Chapter 2** we will outline the biblical foundation for an understanding that every believer is called and equipped for ministry. We will draw on the experience of one congregation that implemented a culture of lay empowerment to demonstrate how to achieve this change, as well as characteristics and challenges that are part of the process.

Each chapter will include a section detailing how to implement the material covered. In **Chapter 3** we discuss the paradigm shift from programs and building to a clear Purpose & Identity for your church, each ministry and each individual. We will use "Church Type/Values Matrix" and prayerful discernment to create or modify your purpose and identity into a compelling vision. For each ministry, we will use covenants with the church's executive council. For each member, we will provide tools to define their individual purpose and unique ministries. To grow their empowerment, we will discuss the elements of an intentional discipleship journey.

To shift the culture, you need a realistic view of what it looks like in your church today—the subject of **Chapter 4**. We have seen the effort to change in many congregations fail simply because they began at the wrong place, unable to accurately assess their current culture. To generate the current state view, we utilize a "What is Church?" exercise combined with a practices survey. The existing culture of individuals is illustrated in an "iceberg model" which emphasizes that mindsets are made up of mental models, values and principles, and fears and needs.

Chapter 5 shows how to shift the culture. The process begins with identifying the specific changes you wish to make based on a desired future state and current state. "Change Readiness Evaluation" and a "Transformation Map" are two critical tools to activate and guide the change. "Cultural Guides" and the "Productive Zone of Disequilibrium" are additional tools for maintaining momentum without falling off the rails.

Chapter 6 addresses the benefits of Shared Leadership. This chapter also enumerates key traits for effective shared leadership. The "Mindsets & Behavior Leadership Model" illustrates the specifics in role modeling, fostering understanding and conviction, developing talent and skills, and reinforcing with formal mechanisms. Covenants and alternative structures are also useful tools for enhanced shared leadership. We will look at biblical models and explore healthy and unhealthy leadership styles and suggest leadership traits that we think are most helpful in leading culture change.

Leaders need followers, so **Chapter 7** explores the challenge of people in the change process. Using the Myers-Briggs Type Indicator we discuss the way personality types influence behavior of both leaders and those they seek to lead. We highlight how different MBTI types react to change, and how they are surprisingly different. From there, we look at the Johari Window to enhance self-awareness during change.

To overcome resistance and barriers to the change process, **Chapter 8** introduces and explores the concepts and tools of Respectable Contrary, the value of conflict, types and layers of resistance, and response to group problems.

Chapter 9 provides some suggestions for caring for leaders who are doing the hard work of culture change. Means to Nurture the Leader's Spirit, Nurture the Leader's Mind, and Nurture the Leader's Body are given. Leading change is unpredictable, and is often messy and chaotic. We show what it means to be an agent for change and how to lead at the edge of chaos at a time when others would retreat.

Chapter 10 invites you to envision what a changed culture might look like for your congregation. We see seven key paradigm shifts essential to a sustained culture change. Implementing the concepts, frameworks, and tools to create and maintain these shifts leads to lasting change. This vastly increases the level of both human and financial resources available to support mission and ministry in your congregation. Several of those paradigm shifts are discussed in earlier chapters, especially the move to lay empowerment described in chapter 2. It is significant that since Andy retired as pastor of Glen Mar Church 13 years ago, three different lead pastors have served the congregation, and yet the culture of called, equipped, and empowered laity continues. Why? Because it was embedded in the laity; they "owned" it. We have found the same experience in creating a culture of generosity in a congregation and will discuss that in some detail.

To illustrate Chapter 10, we offer the story of one congregation's transformation in Appendix B.

Our heart and our focus are on the local congregation, which we consider the front line of the battle for preparing for the coming of God's Kingdom For that reason we will make available to you at no charge all the tools and resources offered in this book. You can simply request them at www.changingchurchculture.com

Through it all we seek to balance the ideas of culture and the framework and tools for change. While aware that many will want to simply try the various tools that we or others propose, we have learned that it is eminently true that culture eats strategy for lunch. In the first two Financial Leadership Academies with which we worked, many recognized experts provided pastors with the latest and greatest tools, but they reported little success in using them to create lasting change. What we discovered, and were able to introduce in the third Academy, was the critical role that culture played in providing either a fertile or unhealthy environment for change. Thus, our focus in this book is on the primacy of partnership in the hard work of leading culture change and in applying frameworks and tools that create lasting change in congregational life and ministries. We pray it will lead you and your congregation to a more fruitful future ministry.

CHAPTER 2
EMPOWERING LAITY FOR MINISTRY

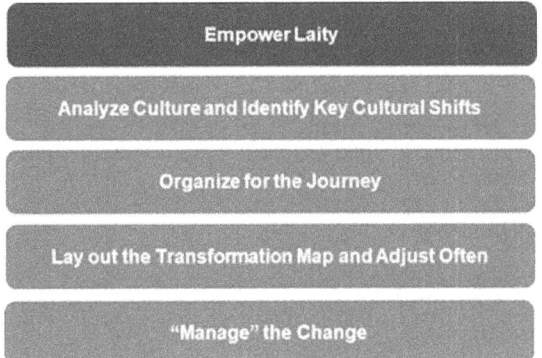

Imagine a church where, when it is time to pray, it is never the pastor who prays—whether in worship, a meeting, or before a meal. It is a church where lay caring ministers wear pagers and are on call 24/7 to respond to pastoral care emergencies. Envision an environment where the majority of the time, a lay person is the one who shows up to pray with you when you are hospitalized or having surgery. See yourself in a faith community where virtually every Bible study, class, or group is led by a trained, gifted lay person. In this community with an average worship attendance of 765, more than 300 persons go on mission trips (local, national, and/or international) every year. Consider how different things might be in your church if almost every ministry in existence originated in the mind of a passionate individual or small group rather than a committee.

This picture likely strikes some as wishful thinking, while others regard it as a hill not worth the climb. The key is that a church like it can and does actually exist. Suffice it to say, the change did not occur overnight. How it reached sustained laity empowerment is a long story filled with pain and struggles (not to mention a pastor who was dragged kicking and screaming every step of the way), and with extensive Bible study and a boatload of mistakes.

Based on Andy's experiences in this particular congregation and our experiences in many others recently, there are some principles that seem to hold hope for a more fruitful future for the ministry of congregations like yours. Now let's look at what might be best described as a journey of discovery with several key markers along the way. Those steps include:

- The Bible Tells Me So
- Every Journey Starts with a Single Step – Prayer
- Minimize Committees
- Many Gifts, One Purpose
- Some Characteristics of Lay Empowerment
    - No Boundaries
    - Permission is Assumed
    - Streamlined Structures
    - Tension between Quality and Participation
    - Things are Getting Messy
- Struggles for Pastors
- Struggles for Laity

THE BIBLE TELLS ME SO

As with anything, it's always good to begin with the basics. And for Christians a return to basics always leads us back to the Bible. Any chance for leading change in the culture of the church that leads to vital ministries and abundant resources must begin with Bible study. In the church where Andy served for 31 years, dramatic culture shifts only became possible following a three-year period marked by congregation-wide, disciplined group Bible study reinforced by preaching. For many congregations, the Bible remains the most underused resource for vitality.

It is in the pages of scripture—both old and new testaments—that we discern God's intention and calling for the church and each individual believer. Beginning as early as the 12th chapter of Genesis, we get a clue to God's intention for the "people of God.

> *Now the Lord said to Abram, "Go from your country and your kindred and your father's house to the land that I will show you. I will make of you a great nation, And I will bless you, and make your name great, so that you will be a blessing…and in you all the families of the earth shall be blessed."*
>
> **Genesis 12:1-3 (NRSV)**

I will bless you **so that you will be a blessing!** The blessing bestowed on Abram was definitely not a reward for past service or merit. Clearly, it was a means of equipping him to carry out God's purpose for him, his family, and the world (all the families of the earth shall be blessed). From the very beginning God called people to accomplish God's purpose by blessing them. The example of Abram remains a lesson for us today. When God gives a blessing, it is never a reward for past service, but always a means of equipping us to serve in the way that God is calling us to serve. The church, and we as individuals, are blessed to be a blessing.

This understanding that we, individually and collectively, are God's people is central to an adequate understanding of the nature of the church. Created by God, shaped by God, we are the instruments for God's purpose being carried out in the world. Throughout history, God has worked to accomplish His purpose through Abraham, through the prophets, and—most fully—through God's own Son, Jesus. Abraham, the prophets, and Jesus of Nazareth, are no longer available as the enablers of God's purpose in the world. Today that role falls to the church, as the body of Christ.

> *And he has put all things under his feet and has made him the head over all things for the church, which is his body, the fullness of him who fills all in all.*
> **Ephesians 1:22-23 (NRSV)**

> *For we are what he has made us, created in Christ Jesus for good works, which God prepared beforehand to be our way of life.*
> **Ephesians 2:10 (NRSV)**

Our purpose, our way of life, is to function as the body of Christ in the world. Not to be a social club, nor primarily a social justice agency, or even simply a purveyor of grace, but the body of Christ. So, the commission Jesus claimed for himself in Luke 4, becomes our commission.

> *The Spirit of the Lord is upon me, because he has anointed me to bring good news to the poor. He has sent me to proclaim release to the captives, and recovery of sight to the blind, to let the oppressed go free, to proclaim the year of the Lord's favor.*
> **Luke 4:18-19 (NRSV)**

Jesus reinforced this when commissioning his original disciples.

> *Go therefore and make disciples of all nations, baptizing them in the name of the Father and of the Son and of the Holy Spirit and teaching them to obey everything that I have commanded you.*
> **Matthew 28:19-20. (NRSV)**

God not only calls us but empowers us as well. Jesus asks the Father to give us another Counselor – the Spirit of Truth - to be with us forever.

> *But you will receive power when the Holy Spirit has come upon you; and you will be my witnesses in Jerusalem, in all Judea and Samaria, and to the ends of the earth*
>
> **Acts 1:8 (NRSV)**

> *And God, who searches the heart, knows what is the mind of the Spirit, because the Spirit intercedes for the saints according to the will of God.*
>
> **Romans 8:27 (NRSV)**

Scripture seems equally clear that ministry is not something reserved for a privileged few, but that every believer is both equipped and expected to serve.

Paul's lengthy description of the nature and role of spiritual gifts in 1 Corinthians 12 emphasizes the importance of the part played by every believer.

> *For the body itself is not made up of only one part, but of many parts. If the foot were to say, "because I am not a hand, I don't belong to the body" that would not keep it from being part of the body. And if the ear were to say, "Because I am not an eye, I don't belong to the body," that would not keep it from being part of the body. If the whole body were just an eye, how could it hear? And if it were only an ear, how could it smell? As it is, however, God put every different part in the body just as God wanted it to be. 1*
>
> **Corinthians 14-18 (NRSV)**

Awakening the sleeping giant in our pews and changing the corporate culture in our churches, requires an acknowledgement that every believer is equipped for ministry in both church and world. When God distributes gifts for ministry, everyone is included, no one is left out. As Paul stresses in Ephesians 4:7, Each one of us has received a special gift in proportion to what Christ has given.

Every single person in your church has been gifted by God to do ministry. The gifts given to ordained clergy are different from—not better than—those given to laity. The key difference, as Ephesians 4:11-12 indicates, is that clergy are gifted to equip rather than to do. ….*He appointed some to be apostles, others to be prophets, others to be evangelists, others to be pastors and teachers. He did this to prepare all God's people for the work of Christian service, in order to build up the body of Christ.* (NRSV)

What a different picture this presents from what plays out in most congregations where it is the clergy and staff who are paid to DO ministry, while members of the congregation either applaud or criticize (depending on individual perspective) their efforts. We have witnessed the results all too well: tired, burned-out clergy, frustrated and marginalized laity, and churches that continue to decline.

While we are spending endless hours agonizing over coming up with the right strategic plan for ministry, God has already laid out the perfect strategic plan. Why is it that we so consistently gravitate to dreaming up our plans and asking God to bless them rather than discerning God's plan for the church that comes to us already blessed?

As mentioned previously, God came to Abraham with the promise that, I will bless you and make your name famous, so that you will be a blessing. (Genesis 12:2). Those two little words, so that, tell the story. God blessed Abraham so that he would be a blessing. God blesses us with spiritual gifts so that we can bless others.

We often get confused about this, thinking that if I am good then God will bless me. But God is not Santa Claus. God's blessing is not a reward, but a call to action. When he was blessed, Abraham had done nothing to distinguish himself. In fact, he had already engaged in some rather disreputable behavior. God did not come to Abraham and say, "because you've been especially good, I will bless you." Instead, it would seem God needed someone to unleash his plan for bringing the world back into relationship with God and Abraham was chosen to do that.

It works the same way in our churches today. God equips every church for the ministry to which it is called by blessing it with gifted clergy and laity. Churches all over are beating themselves up because they don't have the gifts to do what they want to be doing, when God has already equipped them for what God wants them to do.

Maybe we've been guilty of "putting the cart before the horse." We have failed by seeking to first determine our specific mission as a faith community and then searching for the appropriate gifts to accomplish it. Rather, we should first discern the gifts God has given and then determine the mission for which God has equipped us. When God calls an individual or a faith community to do something, God always provides the means for doing it. We need to be spending less time agonizing about how to find ways to resource ministry and more time discerning what God is calling us to do, with the assurance that God has already provided whatever it takes.

The means for fruitful ministry, and for thriving churches, are already in place in our faith communities. And they are imbedded in gifted and called laity who need to be unleashed and empowered to do the things God has blessed them to do.

Every Believer is a Minister

- saved for ministry (2 Tim. 1:9)
- called into ministry (1 Peter 2:9-10)
- gifted for ministry (1 Peter 4:10)
- authorized for ministry (Matt. 28:18-20)
- commanded to minister (Matt. 20:26-28)
- to be prepared for ministry (Eph. 4:11-12)
- needed for ministry (1 Cor. 12:27)
- accountable for ministry (Col. 3:23)

Every Ministry is Important

But in fact God has arranged the parts in the body, every one of them, just as he wanted them to be. If they were all one part, where would the body be? As it is, there are many parts, but one body.

1 Cor 12:18-20 (NIV)

Ministries are dependent on each other

There are different kinds of gifts, but the same Spirit. There are different kinds of service, but the same Lord. There are different kinds of working, but the same God works all of them in all men.

The eye cannot say to the hand, "I don't need you!" And the head cannot say to the feet, "I don't need you!" On the contrary, those parts of the body that seem to be weaker are indispensable,

Now you are the body of Christ, and each one of you is a part of it.
1 Cor 12:18-20 (NIV)

This understanding of the Biblical foundation is essential for changing the culture of a congregation and unleashing the power of called, gifted, and empowered laity.

EVERY JOURNEY BEGINS WITH A SINGLE STEP - PRAYER

Changing the culture of a church is hard work. It takes time, persistence, and lots of prayer. Prayer is often the most underutilized tool in many churches. Any church that is serious about turning around its ministry and empowering laity to do ministry would be well advised to begin with prayer. Pray earnestly. Pray without ceasing. Pray that God will lead you to discern God's purpose for your church and to recognize the gifts that God has already put in place to accomplish that purpose. Prayer is a vital component in changing the culture of a church. And, like so many other components of ministry, it is not something reserved for only pastors.

We know that everyone (well at least they say they do) prays as part of personal devotions. And many families include a prayer before the main meal of the day. But in our experience, there is something about getting more people to pray aloud and in public that can play a huge role in changing the culture of a faith community and help root the understanding that everyone can do ministry. Let us share Andy's story and see if it bears any resemblance to your situation.

When Andy first went to Glen Mar Church as the newly appointed pastor, he was the only one who ever prayed publicly. Whenever it was time for prayer—whether to open a committee meeting, begin a church dinner, and certainly in worship—all eyes would inevitably point to the pastor. Sensing that this was not a healthy situation for any congregation, Andy sought ways to overcome the reluctance in others to pray publicly. Even Andy was surprised by where God led him.

Since he was already meeting many members one-on-one for breakfast or lunch, he began a pattern of saying, "I'll pay but you have to pray." His sense was that if someone could summon the courage to pray in front of the pastor, praying in front of others would seem less daunting.

It cost Andy a ton of money but, over time, the plan began to produce results. At the same time, Andy began to intentionally provide opportunities for some of those folks who had prayed over breakfast or lunch to do so in more public settings. At the close of meetings, he'd announce that attendees could leave as soon as someone was moved to pray. Certainly, the desire to get home overcame any fear about praying aloud. The same thing worked at church dinners. "Well, we can eat as soon as someone is moved to pray." Hunger always won out over fear.

While this may seem like a minor step, we think it represents an entrée into a deeper issue. When only the pastor prays in public, it sends a powerful message that important ministry is reserved for ordained clergy. Once people see others praying, and even experience themselves praying in front of others, it helps to implant the idea that ministry is something everyone can do. When the so-called "pastoral prayer" is offered by a member of the congregation rather than the pastor, it sends a powerful message of inclusive ministry.

MINIMIZE COMMITTEES

With apologies to Marcus Buckingham, whose best-selling books advised readers to **First Break All the Rules**[1] and, in a sequel, to **Now Discover Your Strengths**[2], we'd like to suggest similar advice more suited to churches. We are not advocating breaking all rules, nor ignoring or dismissing past traditions and practices. It will be important to build on the past but not treat it as an idol. Rather, we suggest evaluating standing practices in light of the current purpose (mission) for the church and then be willing to abandon or change those that no longer serve to advance the mission.

It would go something like this: First get rid of all committees except those required by your particular polity or essential to the mission, and then discover your gifts, which we will discuss in the next section.

Committees in the church are the black hole of ministry. Good ideas from passionate people are sent there and, more often than not, never heard from again. By the time a committee considers an idea for ministry and consults with others or refers it to a board for approval, the opportunity may have passed or the individuals with the idea may have lost interest.

There are two basic disadvantages of committees in the church: 1) They consume enormous amounts of time and energy from people who then have little of either left to actually do ministry; and 2) They give a false impression that serving on a committee represents real ministry. A Sunday School team could spend too much time selecting the "perfect" curriculum and too little time coaching and enabling Sunday School teachers.

Now let's be honest. Churches do need a few committees. Someone needs to develop and monitor a budget. Some group needs to hold pastor and staff accountable. And some group needs to provide for orderly succession of members of committees. But, except for a few people whose gifts are administration and organization, serving on a committee is not a ministry for which most folks are gifted and called.

---

[1] Marcus Buckingham & Curt Coffman, *First Break All the Rules: What the World's Greatest Managers Do Differently*, New York, Simon & Schuster 1999

[2] Marcus Buckingham & Donald Clifton, *Now Discover Your Strengths*, New York, The Free Press, 2001

In reality, the majority of the people serving on committees in our churches are there because they couldn't say no. When a member of the congregation's nominating committee, or in some cases the pastor, called to say, "we really need you on this committee," they were afraid they would feel guilty if they declined. But guilt is not a very good motivator for service. The end result is that we get committees populated by people who don't really want to be there.

But there is a second, even greater disadvantage. Well-intentioned committee members spend hours and hours over a period of months coming up with plans for a significant program or event. Then, they have to find someone to actually do the work of making it happen. But no one is left because too many members have been expending all their available time and energy serving on committees.

At one point in Andy's ministry at Glen Mar Church, more than 350 people were serving on committees. Once each month, all the members of every committee would gather in the sanctuary to worship (at least we were smart enough to schedule so that individuals couldn't serve on more than one committee) before going off to their committee meetings. The idea was that beginning with worship together would help focus committee members on the church's purpose and their role in carrying it out. That probably worked, because the committees came up with some really good strategies.

But then, they needed to find people to implement the strategies. With an average worship attendance at the time of around 450, and 350 of them serving on committees, very few people were left with time or energy to implement the grand plans developed in committees. In smaller congregations the ratio is even worse. For example, a Mission Committee could plan an extensive church-wide day of service but then find few able or willing to participate.

You get the idea. If a majority of committed members in any church devote their time to serving on committees, very few people actually get to do hands on ministry. It could be said, we think, that there is an inverse ratio between the number of people serving on committees and the amount of ministry in the world that gets done.

So…what can we do to change this? Well, first, it's not as simple as just getting rid of all committees. Andy learned that the hard way—and hard lessons are often the best lessons since they tend to be more difficult to forget. At a memorable annual meeting of the congregation a motion was made and passed to abolish all committees except those required by the United Methodist Discipline. People were then told, "You are free to pursue the ministry to which you sense God calling you." There was excitement and anticipation of all the ministries that would "bubble up." But nothing happened. Lots of people were relieved, even joyful, that they didn't have to serve on committees for which they had no real interest, let alone passion. But still no ministries resulted.

And so the lesson learned was that in moving toward a lay empowered church, it is not enough to free people to pursue their gifts and calling for ministry. That step is essential, but not sufficient.

Folks who have been consumers of ministry or servers on committees are not going to suddenly become active ministers. They need help, guidance, and ongoing support. The first resource in helping individuals and congregations through this transition is The Bible. Yes, we need to go back to basics again…sometimes we are slow learners. Nothing can substitute for disciplined group Bible study as a means of helping individuals grow to a more mature understanding of the nature of the church and their role in doing ministry.

So, like freeing folks from serving on committees, getting them engaged in Bible study is essential, but not sufficient, to lead them into ministry. The essential is helping each individual—including the pastor—discover their unique gifts for ministry. Many books have been written and multiple systems developed to help individuals identify their spiritual gifts. It is not our purpose to "re-invent the wheel" or to recommend a particular method. Each congregation can choose the method that fits their context best. The important thing is to find and use a good spiritual gifts inventory and then provide the follow-up training and support that will enable individuals to do what God has called them and equipped them to do as ministers.

Armed with an awareness of their spiritual gifts, then, individuals are encouraged to pursue their particular passion for ministry. Very often, if not most of the time, passion and gifts align for ministry. But, instead of having to take a ministry idea to a committee or board for approval, people instead are encouraged to find others who share their passion and do whatever it takes to implement a ministry. Rather than one group planning and then having to find others to implement, there is effectiveness and excitement when the people with passion to do something are the ones who plan, implement, and then evaluate whether it is worth doing again. This is a much better use of time and energy. People end up doing what they want to do, and are passionate about doing, rather than something they were asked to do and couldn't say no.

MANY GIFTS, ONE PURPOSE

As our back-to-basics Bible study has reminded us, everyone has been given gifts by God to equip them for their particular service in carrying out God's purpose for the church. Everyone has been given at least one gift, but no one has been given every gift. Yet we have operated for years as if ordination somehow magically equips a pastor with all the gifts required for ministry. How many pastors have facetiously referred to themselves as a "jack of all trades?"

In virtually every field of endeavor, the day of the generalist is over. What a modern, complex world requires are specialists. When we were growing up every member of the family—from the youngest to the patriarch or matriarch—all went to the same doctor who was almost certainly known as a GP, General Practitioner. Try finding one of those today.

The closest thing to the traditional GP today is likely the area of specialization known as Family Practice. But note…it, too, is an area of specialization. No physician today can be expected to be skilled in every area of medicine.

Yet for reasons that are hard to fathom, churches continue to expect their pastors to be all things to all people—the ecclesiastical equivalent of yesterday's General

Practitioner in medicine. And, sadly, many pastors carry the same expectation of themselves. Worse, some seminaries continue to support that model in their training and course of study. No wonder congregations are frustrated, and pastors are discouraged and burned out. No wonder churches are declining.

The expectation that any—even the most gifted—pastor can be the spiritual GP for a congregation is toxic and must be put away!

In each congregation God has provided all necessary gifts for ministry. But they do not all reside in the pastor! Today's transformational pastor who can lead a faith community to fruitful ministry is one who knows his or her particular gifts. He or she is a pastor who can help members of the flock discover their gifts and lead in ways that maximize the use of those gifts that God has provided to equip the congregation for mission.

Many pastors we know were called to ordination at least partly because of their love for people and desire to help others. They are equipped with great gifts for caring, mercy, and shepherding. These are essential gifts for leading a congregation, but not sufficient for the fullness of fruitful ministry. These pastors should make full use of their great gifts in providing outstanding care for members of their faith community, but they cannot be expected to also be good administrators, teachers, or even—gasp—preachers. But surely God has provided others with those gifts in their congregation.

Other ordained pastors are great preachers, teachers, and visionary leaders. These are the things they should spend most of their time doing while learning to identify, train, and support others who are gifted for other kinds of ministry.

There are many pastors and congregations beginning to take advantage of opportunities to deploy gifted and called laity in forms of pastoral caring—especially through excellent organized ministries like Stephen Ministry. And yet, there is one area that is often neglected as an opportunity for lay ministry. Often the last bastion of clergy privilege, power, and control is worship. Of course laity are expected to serve as ushers, sing in choirs, or perhaps even lead a few responses or read Scripture. But the more central parts of worship are usually reserved for clergy. Having had opportunity to worship in many different churches over the past four years, we can count on the fingers of one hand the number of times we witnessed laity open worship and extend a welcome or offer the pastoral prayer. And, of course, we don't need any fingers on either hand to count the number of times we heard a member of the congregation deliver the sermon. And yet, we're convinced that in many congregations, God has given these gifts to lay members of the faith community.

Don't get us wrong. We believe preaching is an important part of any pastor's calling. Andy taught preaching at Wesley Theological Seminary in Washington, DC for more than 15 years. When greeting each new class he would always say something like, "If God has called you to preach, God has given you gifts for preaching (since God never calls an individual or a congregation to any ministry without providing whatever it takes). My job, and that of your colleagues in this class, is to help you discover your gifts for preaching and learn how to use them most effectively."

But we know (and you do, too) that not all pastors are highly gifted preachers. In many congregations there are laity whose preaching gifts exceed those of the ordained pastor. Refusing to allow them to use their gifts—along with the preaching of the pastor—is a waste and a denial of God's strategic plan for the church. At one time during Andy's 31-year tenure, nearly 25 percent of the preaching was being done by gifted lay members—and no one complained, because it was good preaching!

What we're tapping into, of course, is the historical practice of witnessing, which has become something of a lost art in most congregations today. There is power in hearing the faith of someone like us expressed in a sermon or a prayer. We expect to hear from the pastor—and that is an important element in helping to grow disciples. But by silencing the voice of laity in our congregations we are losing a powerful witness that could do much more to transform the church and the world.

There is, however, one area of ministry no pastor can shirk whether gifted for it or not. That is connecting with the mission field around the church. It is no doubt part of God's sense of humor that a majority of individuals called into ordained ministry are introverts. But having an introverted nature is no excuse to avoid networking in the community. The key for profound introverts is to know that, after time interacting with non-church people (or even people within the church for that matter), we will need alone time to recharge and re-energize.

Jim Griffith regularly says that, "Nothing good happens in the pastor's office." While we can't say we fully agree with this sentiment, we are convinced that every pastor needs to develop the habit of meeting people and being out in the community. As Andy held his one-on-one mentoring meetings with church members at his "branch office," he got to know the wait staff, managers, and other "regulars" for breakfast and lunch. While a few ended up joining the church, most did not. Yet they came to consider Andy their pastor, and would frequently call him aside to talk about some troubling personal issue or to share a particular joy.

In connecting with the mission field, pastors are providing a model for laity that encourages them to do the same. Usually, they are already doing it—and most often better than we can. But seeing the pastor interacting with non-church folks encourages them to see natural networking as an opportunity to connect with others in ways that open doors to sharing their faith and witness in the world.

SOME CHARACTERISTICS OF LAY EMPOWERMENT

Assuming you've been convinced that unleashing the power of lay ministry is a desirable goal for your faith community, what might that look like? What are some of the markers that would indicate the culture is changing and becoming more open and encouraging for laity to use the gifts God has given them for ministry? Based on our experience, there are a few things to keep in mind.

No Boundaries
In many churches the chancel rail (where those still exist) has been a boundary or barrier to the ministry of the laity. Inside the rail is the pastor's domain; outside

is the territory where lay ministry occurs. One of the marks of lay empowerment is greater presence and participation by laity "up front" on stage or inside the chancel area.

A second boundary that disappears is the one that separates ministries that are acceptable and appropriate for clergy from those that are acceptable and appropriate for laity. If we buy (as we obviously do) the argument that God did not discriminate when distributing gifts for things like caring, praying, and preaching, then the field becomes wide open. Anyone who obviously has a gift, whether clergy or lay, should be free to employ that gift in ministry and mission.

Thirdly, laity who are empowered to pursue ministry appropriate to their gifts and calling will discover that this includes ministries that occur "out there" in the world not just "in here" in the church. Many have become accustomed to understanding that ministry is something we do in—or at least for—the church. In reality, if churches and individuals are being faithful to their calling, more ministry will be happening in the world through individuals who may or may not be operating under sponsorship of any faith community. Lay empowerment erases the boundary between church and world.

Permission Is Assumed
The boundary that continues to exist is represented by the purpose, identity, values, and beliefs of the congregation. Any ministry that does not violate one of these is assumed to be permitted. Accountability is inherent in the need for any group proposing a new ministry. They must demonstrate how that particular ministry "fits" into, and helps to carry out, the congregation's purpose. Permission comes from that alignment, rather than through the approval of a standing committee or board. Of course, that assumes the congregation has a clearly stated purpose.

Streamlined Structures
A congregation that is committed to lay empowerment will have just enough structure to support ministry. Too much structure inhibits ministry by consuming so much time and energy that little is left over for doing ministry. The goal is to

free people to devote their time and energy to hands on ministry, as well as to have form follow function.

So…how much is enough? How many boards and/or committees does a faith community need in order to minister effectively? To answer that question, let's talk about an element in paradigm shift from structure focus to missional focus, from programs and building to purpose & identity.

The traditional mental model for the church hierarchy is:

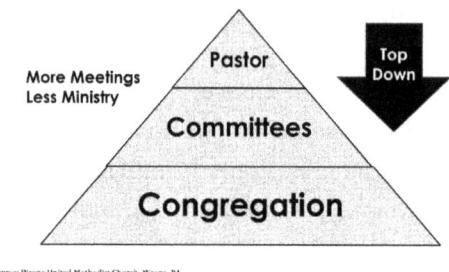

This results in many committees and many meetings. Lots of talk and planning and, on the whole, little action. New members often get swept up into this, thinking they are serving God through committee membership.

The alternative mental model is:

The pastors and laity leaders are equipping and coaching members to have a missional focus, be kingdom builders versus kingdom dwellers, and serve the community and other church members versus serving on committees.

Clearly, some structure is needed to provide overall vision and direction. Every congregation will need a church council or board. But that group certainly does not need to meet monthly. In our experience, four to six meetings each year should be sufficient to accomplish the responsibilities of the council, which are primarily to assure alignment of the congregation's resources with its purpose and mission. Budgets and funding plans must be approved, progress toward goals that implement the purpose should be evaluated, and staff must be hired and deployed.

In addition to the council/board, a finance committee is likely needed to oversee the development and month to month performance of the budget and funding. A pastor parish or staff parish committee will handle staffing and accountability for the paid staff. Recruitment and deployment of those who are unpaid would fall to a nominating or leadership development committee. These administrative committees may be sufficient for many congregations.

Some churches may want to have committees for things like worship, Christian learning, or mission. But it will usually be much better to simply entrust these functions to task groups or ministry teams who are actually involved in these areas. At Glen Mar, for example, there were worship teams for each of the four distinct worship services. For the most part, they spoke different languages and had different priorities suited to the individual service in which they participated. Asking one overall group to take responsibility for services that ran the gamut from informal to traditional to cutting edge contemporary would have been to invite disaster. With a narrower focus, ministry teams can meet, plan, and evaluate more effectively.

Churches don't need committees spending their time and energy deciding what and how others should function in ministry. Andy will never forget his own first experience with what was then called an administrative board. Fresh out of seminary, with passion and excitement for transforming the world, he endured a 90-minute meeting in which a full two-thirds of the time was spent in discussing whether to continue or change the ratio of hard candy to chocolates in the children's Easter baskets. It almost drove him away from ministry. But it did create a lasting impression and conviction that much of the time and energy expended in church meetings would be better spent in ministry.

Tension Between Quality and Participation

Any church that gets serious about changing its culture to becoming more supportive of lay empowerment will need to be ready for tension and conflict. Remember when we said it would be hard work? One of the more troublesome areas of tension that may arise early occurs when people begin to question whether "allowing" laity to engage in more public ministries will diminish the quality and excellence to which they've become accustomed. This stems, of course, from an unspoken assumption that quality and excellence come only from "professionals."

The answer is both "no" and "yes." No, quality will not diminish because we are not sending just anyone to visit in the hospital, pray, lead worship, or preach, but individuals who have been found to be gifted for these tasks. Further, we will have provided some level of training and practice before their first public engagement. And, as most congregations will discover, the visits, prayers, and even sermons of gifted laity are more excellent than those of clergy who are not equally gifted in those areas.

But the answer is also yes. There is always a learning curve for anyone engaging in something new. An individual's first "pastoral prayer" may lack some of the polish of the pastor. In time, though, a truly gifted person will become more excellent in the practice of the ministry for which they have been given gifts.

Nevertheless, the pastor who is leading a congregation in transforming the culture to one of greater lay empowerment will have to contend with questions of quality and will need to be committed to valuing participation at least as highly as professionalism. In such an environment intention, authenticity, and heart trump perfection.

Things are Getting Messy Around Here

One of the greatest obstacles to moving a congregation toward greater lay empowerment arises with the realization that things appear to be getting out of control. When new structures and new ways of doing ministry begin to appear and grow, many will want to abandon the wilderness of lay empowerment for the Egypt of the way we've always done it. This can be especially true for pastors who—in the United Methodist system, at any rate—are ordained to a ministry of word, sacrament, and *Order*.

In reality, lay ministry is anything but orderly. From most perspectives, it would be better described as messy and chaotic. It appears that no one is in charge. And, with so many new ministries emerging—both in the church and in the community—it becomes impossible for anyone to know everything that is happening. For pastors who aspire to be in control (admit it, a high percentage of pastors fall into that infamous category of "control freaks!") it can be downright devastating.

Andy will never forget the first time he ran head on into this realization. He was leading a workshop with the congregation's lay leader at the time. The topic of this workshop was none other than lay empowerment. This was early in the process when we hadn't yet realized how much we still didn't know. Andy was discussing how members of a local mission team had been talking with the county about how churches might do something to help the growing homeless population. As he explained that we hoped to initiate a rotating cold weather shelter sometime within the next few months, the lay leader leaned over and said, "Andy, we're hosting the first shelter next week." And this was the first of many more amazing surprises!

Armed with a sense of their calling and a passion for helping homeless persons in the community, this team of individuals had taken seriously what they'd been told about permission being assumed. They never went to a mission committee (which didn't exist of course), church council, or even trustees for approval. Fortunately, they did coordinate with the other ministry teams whose events would be displaced during the time the "annex" was being used as a cold weather shelter. The sense of calling and the assumption of permission enabled them to move quickly to meet an immediate need. Imagine how much longer the process would have taken if the idea had to make its way through the normal channels of church bureaucracy! But even the lead pastor was not fully aware of what was happening in the process.

If ministry is limited to what can be controlled, there will be an absolute limit to the number and extent of ministries a church can provide. If the only ministries allowed are those about which the pastor has full information and hands-on influence, many ministries will remain still-born and pressing needs will go unmet. In contrast, unleashing laity to follow their God-given gifts and passion for serving can enable the number and extent of ministries to grow almost exponentially.

But, make no mistake about it; there is a price to pay. And the price is learning to live in a less orderly, more messy, and chaotic environment—something like the Kingdom of God described in many of Jesus' parables. It might be good for those of us who seek order and control to be reminded from time to time that, "the Spirit blows where it wills."

So, one might well ask, where does accountability lie in such a different environment? The answer for us lies in two places. First, in reality, someone is in control. God is in control. Through the distribution of gifts and callings to a particular faith community, God is determining what ministries happen. How wonderfully freeing for a congregation to stop spending endless and agonizing hours wondering how to find the means to accomplish their goals and to know that God has already provided the means to do whatever He is calling them to do.

Secondly, accountability is to the purpose, identity and context of the particular faith community. These provide the boundaries, if you will, for a kind of playing field on which ministry takes place. Individual teams of people who sense they are called and gifted design and implement the plays, rather than a committee or board sitting on the sidelines. But each team understands that their "play" needs to stay within the bounds of the beliefs and values of the faith community and to "advance the ball" in the direction of their shared vision and mission.

Some will see this as too loose and wonder who plays the role of referee to call a ministry "out of bounds." Once again, the Bible provides an answer. The formula advises going quietly to the offending party. And, in reality, this becomes one of the responsibilities for the pastor and leadership team or church council. But their role is one of alignment rather than permission giving in advance. Our conviction is that teaching, preaching, and modeling purpose, identity and context create the kind of corporate culture in which people come to know what is in bounds and what is not. This goes along with consistent and intentional efforts to convey the essence of gifted and called laity empowered for ministry.

STRUGGLES FOR THE PASTOR

The first person to notice a change when a congregation begins to move toward greater empowerment of laity, will inevitably be the pastor. Most pastors are drawn to ordained ministry by a desire to help people, to make a difference in the lives of individuals and communities. These are certainly positive and admirable motivations. But between the ideal and the implementation, there are at least two dangerous pitfalls that can trap the unsuspecting pastor. First, is a growing need to be in control. While most pastors would stop short of proclaiming "my way or the highway," there is a definite tendency to conclude that their time and investment in training gives them the sole authority to call the shots. We not only know what should be done in the ministries of a congregation, but also how they ought to be accomplished.

It is not difficult at all for pastors to find themselves with a powerful desire to be the star quarterback who calls the signals and directs every aspect of the church's ministry. And many congregations feed and encourage that desire by indicating in no uncertain terms that it is their expectation of the pastor as well. This is clearly characteristic of what has been dubbed the "pastor-centered church." The problem, though, is that many pastors and congregations that have grown to a size where this style is no longer effective still follow it as the model for their ministry. This inevitably leads to a pastor who burns out or becomes increasingly discouraged because she/he cannot possibly do everything they and the congregation expect them to be doing.

But there is also a second, and in some ways even more insidious, temptation for pastors. It grows out of the fact that ministry provides very little in the way of objective feedback or evaluation for one's efforts. Annual evaluations have the potential, but they can all too easily become gauges of popularity rather than effectiveness. The reality is that, day-to-day, there is very little opportunity for the conscientious pastor to gauge how am I doing? in ministry. As a result, many pastors will find themselves working as hard as possible, with the thought that if I'm always busy, I must be accomplishing something positive.

This is certainly the trap Andy fell into as a young pastor. His family suffered, his physical and emotional health suffered. Still, he at least convinced himself that his ministry was worth something. The dangerous trap for pastors (and for all in every occupation to some extent) is that our sense of self-worth is tied to what we do. So when a pastor finds her or himself in a situation where they are suddenly doing less, the temptation is great to conclude they are worth less.

And, unintentionally, Andy ended up limiting the opportunity for the congregation to reach new people and to grow. If he had to be the one doing virtually everything, that placed an absolute limit on the total amount of ministry that could be accomplished. By God's grace he, and the congregation, were led to discover that his worth as pastor was related not to what he personally could do, but to the amount of ministry that could be accomplished by all working together for the church's mission.

Pastors want to be important and useful. And we want to be liked. Giving up doing many of the things we have always done can seriously threaten our sense of both self-worth and acceptance. What is required, though, is a transition which God can work in us. We go from finding worth in what we do personally to finding worth in what the congregation does using their collective gifts for ministry. Along with this comes another transition as well, from concern about how members of the faith community relate with us to our primary concern about how they relate to God and to the community outside the church. These are things that God will provide as we seek to follow His strategic plan for the church. Leading this kind of culture shift will most likely result in some loss of members who are not inclined to be more actively engaged in ministry. In time, though, the congregation will grow with those who are attracted by the opportunity to employ their gifts in hands-on ministries. In addition, much of what we are suggesting may be contrary to what judicatory officials expect. It will be important for the transformational pastor leader to meet in advance with supervisors to explain the new direction and, hopefully, gain their support.

STRUGGLES FOR LAITY

Just as pastors will experience the stress of "giving up" ministry as a congregation moves toward greater lay empowerment, laity will encounter their own struggles with "taking up" more meaningful ministry in the life of the church. Most will have been conditioned over many years to expect and accept a more passive role in the life of the church. Many will have come to equate serving on committees as the best form of ministry available to them. A few may have dipped a toe gingerly into the shallow waters of hands-on ministry by going on a mission trip or volunteering to read scripture in worship. Most, however, will not have ventured into the deeper waters of more "professional" or "pastoral" kinds of ministry. And, of course, this is one of those places where the so-called "seven last words of the church" are likely to be heard. The pastor and leaders are almost certain to be confronted with claims that, "We've never done it this way before," or "We've always done it that way before."

Another struggle for laity will come when they are encouraged to consider that ministry is not something that happens only in the church. The thought that they can be in ministry where they work, play, or socialize may be entirely foreign and more than a little frightening for folks who have long regarded ministry as something we do "at church."

So, when invited to "come up higher" in the hierarchy of ministry, most folks will find themselves at something of a loss. Even if Bible study and preaching have convinced them that ministry is something for which God has given everyone gifts and calling, they will likely lack enough confidence to give it a try. This is understandable for anyone venturing into a new endeavor. Some may have picked up an attitude of "damn the torpedoes, full speed ahead," and will forge ahead heedless of potential dangers. But for most, there will be a need for intentional training, mentoring, and encouragement before they gain sufficient confidence to "give it a try."

One of the best ways to accomplish this is for the visionary pastor to identify individuals who are "spiritually pregnant." These are people who are actively called by the Spirit to a particular ministry. The pastor must then invest significant one-on-one time, helping them to allow God to give birth to their new ministry. This calls for the pastor to serve as a kind of spiritual mid-wife. Eventually, some of these individuals will move on to repeat the same process with others, so that the pastor can then begin to mentor leaders who will recruit and mentor other leaders.

A good process for moving in this direction could be something like the so-called "leadership square" or "discipleship square"[3].

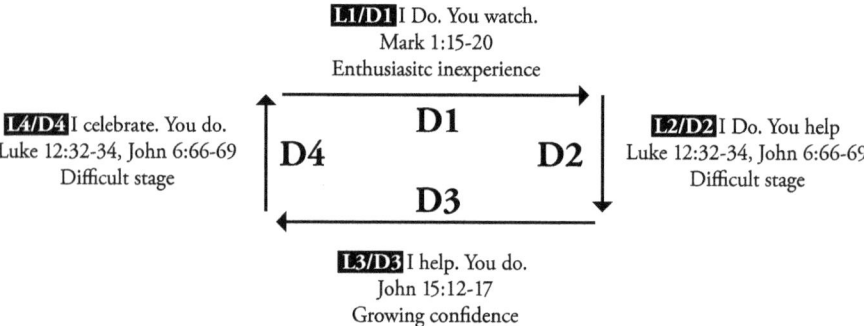

As with conversion to belief itself, for some this will be a dramatic and sudden realization, while for others the process will be more slow and gradual. Eventually, though, if God has given gifts for and is calling someone into some form of ministry, and if they are encouraged and mentored in that direction, they will "get it."

LIVE IT OUT

- If you are the pastor, design and implement a study and sermon series focused on the ministry of all believers.

- Choose one area of ministry in which to empower laity. Create a plan to recruit, train, and support lay ministers.

- Identify a spiritual gifts inventory that best suits your congregation.

---

[3] The Discipleship Square: Multiplying Disciples, adapted from Mike Breen, *Multiplying Missional Leaders*, Pawleys Island, SC, 3DM, 2012

CHAPTER 2
EMPOWERING LAITY FOR MINISTRY TOOLS

The process of leading lasting change in any congregation requires a partnership between laity and clergy. Laity who have been passive spectators or followers may not understand that they—as much as clergy—are called and equipped for ministry. Indeed, Jesus sent the Holy Spirit to fill his followers with comfort, advice, courage, and strength.

Here are some tools to help laity discover, develop, and deploy their unique gifts for ministry:
- Discovering How God Has Shaped Me for Ministry*
- Intentional Discipleship
- Covenants

The prayer and scripture are offered for spiritual grounding as you use these tools.

---

* A PDF version of this tool can be requested at www.changingchurchculture.com

PRAYER

Lord God, you know me better than I know myself. You know my innermost being, my thoughts and desires. And you have created me in your image and given me gifts that I might serve you and others in your name. Lead me to understand that I am blessed to be a blessing, and show me the way to employ the gifts you have given to build up the body of Christ and work toward the unity of the faith. Through Jesus Christ our living Savior. Amen.

SCRIPTURE

It was He who gave some to be apostles, some to be prophets, some to be evangelists, and some to be pastors and teachers, to prepare God's people for works of service, so that the body of Christ may be built up until we all reach unity in the faith and in the knowledge of the Son of God and become mature, attaining to the whole measure of the fullness of Christ.

Ephesians 4:11-13

The pastor necessarily plays a key role in empowering laity for ministry. An authoritarian pastor who needs a great measure of control makes lay empowerment difficult, if not impossible.

If you are a pastor, we suggest you begin by identifying potential leaders among laity in the congregation. Then initiate a series of one-on-one meetings to discuss your vision for lay empowerment and encourage them to consider their gifts for leadership. Once you have identified and recruited a number of potential leaders, engage them as a group in the following exercises.

DISCOVERING HOW GOD HAS SHAPED ME FOR MINISTRY

This is a six-part exercise. It can be done in one session or broken up into six parts that are done as part of a regular committee/ministry meeting.

PART A
Ask each participant to fill in the blanks.

GREAT COMMANDMENT

"The most important one," answered Jesus is this: Hear, O Israel, the LORD our God, the LORD is _____,"
Mark 12:29

"Love the LORD your God with all your _____, and with all your _____, with all your _____, and with all your _____,
Mark 12:30

The second is this: 'Love your _____ as yourself.' There is no commandment greater than these."
Mark 12:31

GREAT COMMISSION

"Then Jesus came to them and said, "All authority in heaven and on earth has been given to me. Therefore, go and make _____ of all nations, baptizing them in the name of the Father and of the Son and of the Holy Spirit, and teaching them to obey everything I have commanded you. And surely I am with you always, to the very end of the age."
Matthew 28:18-20

PART A (ANSWER SHEET)

GREAT COMMANDMENT

"The most important one," answered Jesus is this: Hear, O Israel, the LORD our God, the LORD is **One**,"
Mark 12:29

"Love the LORD your God with all your **heart**, and with all your **soul**, with all your **mind**, and with all your **strength**,
Mark 12:30

The second is this: 'Love your **neighbor** as yourself.' There is no commandment greater than these."
Mark 12:31

GREAT COMMISSION

"Then Jesus came to them and said, "All authority in heaven and on earth has been given to me. Therefore, go and make **disciples** of all nations, baptizing them in the name of the Father and of the Son and of the Holy Spirit, and teaching them to obey everything I have commanded you. And surely I am with you always, to the very end of the age."
Matthew 28:18-20

Read the following and discuss as a group.

THE BIBLICAL BASIS FOR EVERY MEMBER MINISTRY

Every believer is a minister.
Every Christian is

- created for ministry (Eph. 2:10)
- saved for ministry (2 Tim. 1:9)
- called into ministry (1 Peter 2:9-10)
- gifted for ministry (1 Peter 4:10)
- authorized for ministry (Matt. 28:18-20)
- commanded to minister (Matt. 20:26-28)
- to be prepared for ministry (Eph. 4:11-12)
- needed for ministry (1 Cor. 12:27)
- accountable for ministry (Col. 3:23-24)

Every Ministry is important.
But in fact God has arranged the parts in the body, every one of them, just as he wanted them to be. If they were all one part, where would the body be? As it is, there are many parts, but one body.
1 Cor. 12:18-20

Ministries are dependent on each other.
There are different kinds of gifts, but the same Spirit. There are different kinds of service, but the same Lord. There are different kinds of working, but the same God works all of them in all men.
The eye cannot say to the hand, "I don't need you!" And the head cannot say to the feet, "I don't need you!" On the contrary, those parts of the body that seem to be weaker are indispensable,
Now you are the body of Christ, and each one of you is a part of it.
1 Cor. 12: 4-6, 21-22, 27

Ministry is the expression of a person's SHAPE[4]

The five elements of SHAPE are spiritual gifts, heart, abilities, personality, and experiences.

Introduce SHAPE through definitions and illustrations in Paul's life.

SPIRITUAL GIFTS

> ...But each man has his own gift from God; one has this gift, another has that.
>
> 1 Corinthians 7:7

HEART

> For God has put it into their hearts to accomplish his purpose...
>
> Rev 17:17

ABILITIES

> There are different kinds of working, but the same God works all of them in all men.
>
> 1 Cor. 12:6

PERSONALITY

> For who among men knows the thoughts of a man except the man's spirit within him? In the same way no one knows the thoughts of God except the Spirit of God.
>
> 1 Cor. 2:11

EXPERIENCE

> God...comforts us in all our troubles, so that we can comfort those in any trouble with the comfort we ourselves have received from God.
>
> 2 Cor. 1:4

---

[4]Chapter 19 – Turning Members into Ministers, The Purpose Driven Church, Growth without Compromising Your Message & Mission by Rick Warren, Zondervan, Grand Rapids, Michigan, 1995

HOW PAUL'S MINISTRY WAS SHAPED

Paul's Spiritual Gifts
And of this gospel I was appointed a herald and an apostle and a teacher. 2 Tim. 1:11-12

Paul's Heart
It has always been my ambition to preach the gospel where Christ was not known, so that I would not be building on someone else's foundation.
Rom. 15:20-21

Paul's Ability
Paul went to see them, and because he was a tentmaker as they were, he stayed and worked with them. Every Sabbath he reasoned in the synagogue, trying to persuade Jews and Greeks.
Acts 18:2b-4

Paul's Personality
For you have heard of my previous way of life in Judaism, how intensely I persecuted the church of God and tried to destroy it. I was advancing in Judaism beyond many Jews of my own age and was extremely zealous for the traditions of my fathers.
Gal. 1:13-14

Paul's Experiences
Spiritual
- Watching Stephen be stoned (Acts 8:1)
- Conversion on the Damascus Road (Acts 9:1-20
- Three years maturing in Arabia (Gal 1:18)
- Special vision from God (2 Cor. 12:2-7)

Painful

To keep me from becoming conceited because of these surpassingly great revelations, there was given me a thorn in my flesh, a messenger of Satan, to torment me.

2 Cor. 12:7

Educational

I am a Jew, born in Tarsus of Cilicia, but brought up in this city. Under Gamaliel I was thoroughly trained in the law of our fathers and was just as zealous for God as any of you are today.

Acts 22:3

Ministry

Book of Acts

PART B
DISCOVERING HOW GOD HAS SHAPED ME FOR MINISTRY

SPIRITUAL GIFTS

Now about spiritual gifts, brothers, I do not want you to be ignorant.

1 Cor. 12:1

Review and discuss this background information which will be useful in Parts C, D, E, and F.

TEN TRUTHS

1. Only believers have spiritual gifts.

The man without the Spirit does not accept the things that come from the Spirit of God, for they are foolishness to him, and he cannot understand them, because they are spiritually discerned.

1 Cor. 2:14

2. Every Christian has at least one gift.

I wish that all men were as I am. But each man has his own gift from God; one has this gift, another has that.

1 Cor. 7:7

3. No one receives all the gifts.

Now you are the body of Christ, and each one of you is a part of it. And in the church God has appointed first of all apostles, second prophets, third teachers, then workers of miracles, also those having gifts of healing, those able to help others, those with gifts of administration, and those speaking in different kinds of tongues. Are all apostles? Are all prophets? Are all teachers? Do all work miracles? Do all have gifts of healing? Do all speak in tongues? Do all interpret?

1 Cor. 12:27-30

4. No single gift is given to everyone. 1 Cor. 12:29-30

Are all apostles? Are all prophets? Do all work miracles? Do all have gifts of healing? Do all speak in tongues? Do all interpret?

1 Cor. 12:29-30

5. You can't earn/work for a spiritual gift.

But to each one of us grace has been given as Christ apportioned it.

Eph 4:7

6. The Holy Spirit decides what gifts I get.

All these are the work of one and the same Spirit, and he gives them to each one, just as he determines.

1 Cor. 12:11

7. The gifts I'm given are permanent.

...for God's gifts and his call are irrevocable

Rom. 11:29

8. I am to develop the gifts God gives me.

Do not neglect your gift, which was given you through a prophetic message when the body of elders laid their hands on you.

Rom. 11:29

9. It's a sin to waste the gifts God gave me.

So then, men ought to regard us as servants of Christ and as those entrusted with the secret things of God. Now it is required that those who have been given a trust must prove faithful.

1 Cor. 4:1-2

Matthew 25: 14-30 *Parable of the Talents*

10. Using my gifts glorifies God and grows me.

This is to my Father's glory, that you bear much fruit, showing yourselves to be my disciples.

John 15:8

THE PURPOSE OF SPIRITUAL GIFTS

a. Not for my benefit, but for others.

Each one should use whatever gift he has received to serve others, faithfully administering God's grace in its various forms.

1 Peter 4:10

b. To produce unity and maturity in our church family.

It was he who gave 'gifts to men' so that the body of Christ may be built up until we all reach unity in the faith and in the knowledge of the Son of God and become mature, attaining to the whole measure of the fullness of Christ. Then we will no longer be infants, tossed back and forth by the waves, and blown here and there by every wind ….

Rom. 11:29

CAUTIONS ABOUT SPIRITUAL GIFTS

- Don't confuse gifts with natural talents.
- Don't confuse gifts with the Fruit of the Spirit
    - Fruits show my maturity – Galatians 5:22
    - Gifts show my ministry
- Be aware of the dangers of "gift projection," i.e. expecting others to serve the way you do and have similar results.
- Don't feel that my gift makes me superior to others 1 Cor. 12:21
- Realize that using my gift without love is worthless 1 Cor. 13:1-13

UNWRAPPING YOUR GIFTS

The Bible has four major lists of gifts:

Romans 12:3-8
For by the grace given me I say to every one of you: Do not think of yourself more highly than you ought, but rather think of yourself with sober judgment, in accordance with the measure of faith God has given you. Just as each of us has one body with many members, and these members do not all have the same function, so in Christ we who are many form one body, and each member belongs to all the others. We have different gifts, according to the grace given us. If a man's gift is prophesying, let him use it in proportion to his faith. If it is serving, let him serve; if it is teaching, let him teach; if it is encouraging, let him encourage; if it is contributing to the needs of others, let him give generously; if it is leadership, let him govern diligently; if it is showing mercy, let him do it cheerfully.

1 Corinthians 12:1-11, 27-31
Now about spiritual gifts, brothers, I do not want you to be ignorant. You know that when you were pagans, somehow or other you were influenced and led astray to mute idols. Therefore I tell you that no one who is speaking by the Spirit of God says, "Jesus be cursed," and no one can say, "Jesus is Lord," except by the Holy Spirit.

There are different kinds of gifts, but the same Spirit. There are different kinds of service, but the same Lord. There are different kinds of working, but the same God works all of them in all men.

Now to each one the manifestation of the Spirit is given for the common good. To one there is given through the Spirit the message of wisdom, to another the message of knowledge by means of the same Spirit, to another faith by the same Spirit, to another gifts of healing by that one Spirit, to another miraculous powers, to another prophecy, to another distinguishing between spirits, to another speaking in different kinds of tongues, and to still another the interpretation of tongues. All these are the work of one and the same Spirit, and he gives them to each one, just as he determines.

Now you are the body of Christ, and each one of you is a part of it. And in the church God has appointed first of all apostles, second prophets, third teachers, then workers of miracles, also those having gifts of healing, those able to help others, those with gifts of administration, and those speaking in different kinds of tongues. Are all apostles? Are all prophets? Are all teachers? Do all work miracles? Do all have gifts of healing? Do all speak in tongues? Do all interpret? But eagerly desire the greater gifts.

Ephesians 4:11-12
It was he who gave some to be apostles, some to be prophets, some to be evangelists, and some to be pastors and teachers, to prepare God's people for works of service, so that the body of Christ may be built up.

1 Peter 4:9-11
Offer hospitality to one another without grumbling. Each one should use whatever gift he has received to serve others, faithfully administering God's grace in its various forms. If anyone speaks, he should do it as one speaking the very words of God. If anyone serves, he should do it with the strength God provides, so that in all things God may be praised through Jesus Christ. To him be the glory and the power for ever and ever.

PART C
DISCOVERING HOW GOD HAS SHAPED ME FOR MINISTRY
Monitoring my heartbeat & Applying my abilities

MONITORING MY HEARTBEAT

The Bible uses the term "heart" to represent the center of your motivation, desires, and inclinations.

Ps 37:4
Delight yourself in the LORD and he will give you the desires of your heart.

God has given each of us a unique emotional "heartbeat". We instinctively feel deeply about some things and not about others. It's what motivates us to pursue certain activities and subjects that really interest us.

Why has God given each of us a unique "heartbeat"?

Rev 17:17
For God has put it into their hearts to accomplish his purpose.....

1 Sam 12:20
.... serve the LORD with all your heart.

Eph 6:6-7
.... doing the will of God from your heart.

SPIRITUAL EKG

If you are like most people, you have never taken time to sort out and identify the things you are motivated to accomplish. The key to understanding your "heartbeat" is to look at your past accomplishments.

---

[5]Finding a Job You Can Love by Ralph T Mattson and Arthur F Miller, Jr, P&R Publishing, Phillipsburg, NJ, 1999

This exercise is adapted from the book Finding a Job You Can Love.[5]

What to include:
1. Accomplishments at home, school, work, etc.
2. Things you enjoyed doing.
3. Things you believe you did well.
4. Give specific details about what you did.
5. Forget what other people think about it.

STEP 1:
List and Describe Your Accomplishments Since Childhood

1. Remember, list things you enjoyed doing and did well, not simply pleasant experiences.

   Bad Example: Had a great vacation in Canada

   Good Example: Took postcard-quality photos during my vacation

2. You don't have to cover every year of your life. Just focus on what you feel are the highlights of things you've done.

My Grade School Years

1. _____
_____
2. _____
_____

As a Teenager

1. _____
_____
2. _____
_____

In College or Early 20's

1._____
_____
2._____
_____
3._____
_____
4._____
_____

In my "Thirty-something Years"

1._____
_____
2._____
_____
3._____
_____
4._____
_____

Up to the Present

1._____
_____
2._____
_____
3._____
_____
4._____
_____

STEP 2:
Discover the Motivated Direction of Your Heart

Examine your achievements for a common motivational thread. You might find a key phrase repeated. See if you can match one of the heartbeats listed below.

Remember these are ALL God-given motivations. They are only sinful when used selfishly. Every one of these can be used in effective ministry. Don't be embarrassed to identify a basic heartbeat that doesn't seem spiritual. Almost every one of these can be identified in the ministry of one of the twelve Apostles.

DESIGN/DEVELOP – I love to make something out of nothing. I enjoy getting something started from scratch.

PIONEER – I love to test and try out new concepts. I am not afraid to risk failure.

ORGANIZE – I love to bring order out of chaos. I enjoy organizing something that is already started.

OPERATE/MAINTAIN – I love to efficiently maintain something that is already organized.

SERVE/HELP – I love to assist others in their responsibilities. I enjoy helping others succeed.

ACQUIRE/POSSESS – I love to shop, collect, or obtain things. I enjoy getting the highest quality for the best price.

EXCEL – I love to be the best and make my team the best. I enjoy setting and attaining the highest standard.

INFLUENCE – I love to convert people to my way of thinking. I enjoy shaping the attitudes and behavior of others.

PERFORM – I love to be on stage and receive the attention of others. I enjoy being in the limelight.

IMPROVE – I love to make things better. I enjoy taking something that someone else has designed or started and improve it.

REPAIR – I love to fix what is broken or change what is out of date.

PERSEVERE – I love to see things to completion. I enjoy persisting at something until it is finished.

FOLLOW THE RULES – I love to operate by policies and procedures. I enjoy meeting the expectations of an organization or boss.

PREVAIL – I love to fight for what is right and oppose what is wrong. I enjoy overcoming injustice.

I feel the basic motivation god has put in my heart is to:

My history supports this condition with these examples:

-
-

APPLYING MY ABILITIES

One of the most common reasons people give for not getting involved in ministry is, "I don't have any abilities to offer."

Misconceptions About Abilities

1. **MYTH**: Skills which must be learned are learned primarily in the classroom. Actually, some of your most basic skills were learned at home, 'in the street', or somewhere else outside the classroom.

2. **MYTH**: If you have certain abilities, you will be very aware that you have them. This is not true. You are probably using a number of talents or skills that you are not even aware of. Ask others.

3. **MYTH**: Skills that I use at work are usable only in that environment. I couldn't use them in ministry. Hopefully, you will see this is not true.

4. **MYTH**: Most people only have a very few abilities. National studies have proven that the average person possesses hundreds of skills.

Discovering Your Abilities

Look over your list of accomplishments again. Circle the verbs that denote actions and compare them to the list below.

Ability	Definition	Check if you have this ability
Entertaining	Perform, act, dance, speak, magic tricks	
Recruiting	Elist and motivate people to get involved	
Interviewing	Discover what others are really like	
Researching	Read, gather information, collect data	
Artistic	Conceptualize, picture, draw, paint, photograph, or make renderings	

Ability	Definition	Check if you have this ability
Graphics	layout, design, create visual displays or banners	
Evaluating	Analyze data and draw conclusions	
Planning	Strategize, design, and organize programs & events	
Managing	Supervise people to accomplish a task or event and coordinate the details involved	
Couseling	Listen, encourage, and guide with sensitivity	
Teaching	Explain, train, demonstrate, tutor	
Writing	Write articles, letters, books	
Editing	Proofread or rewrite	
Promoting	Advertise or promote events and activities	
Repairing	Fix, restore, maintain	
Feeding	Create meals for large or small groups	
Recall	Remember or recall names and faces	
Mechanical Operating	Operate equipment, tools or machinery	
Resourceful	Search out and find inexpensive materials or resources needed	
Counting	Work with numbers, data, or money	
Classifying	Systematize and file books, data, records, and materials so they can be retrieved easily	
Public Relations	Handle complaints and unhappy customers with care and courtesy	
Welcoming	Convey warmth, develop rapport, make others feel comfortable	
Composing	Write music or lyrics	
Landscaping	Gardening and work with plants	
Decorating	Beautify a setting for a special event	
Computing	Set up, maintain, and repair computer systems	
Internet	Set up, maintain, and improve web pages	
Audio-Visual Display	Use of audio and visual presentation tools to enhance events and communicate	

What's your current vocation?

_____

What primary skill(s) do you use in it?

_____

What have been previous vocation(s)?

_____

What skill(s) did you use in them?

_____

I feel I have the following abilities:

_____

_____

_____

PART D
DISCOVERING HOW GOD HAS SHAPED ME FOR MINISTRY

EXAMINING MY EXPERIENCES

One of the most overlooked factors in determining the ministry God has for me is past experience, particularly my hurts and problems I've overcome with God's help. Since our greatest life messages come out of our weaknesses and not our strengths, we should pay close attention to what we've learned in the "school of hard knocks".

God never wastes a hurt. He wants you to be open to ministering to people who are going through what you've already been through.

Praise be to the God and Father of our Lord Jesus Christ, the Father of compassion and the God of all comfort, who comforts us in all our troubles, so that we can comfort those in any trouble with the comfort we ourselves have received from God.

2 Cor 1:3-4

Reflect and write about these experiences:

Your spiritual experiences

Your painful experiences

Your educational experiences

Your ministry experiences

PART E
DISCOVERING HOW GOD HAS SHAPED ME FOR MINISTRY

HABITS FOR SPIRITUAL GROWTH

Devotion: Imitation Christ's Humility
Philippians 2:1-11

Purpose:

Col 4:12
He is always wrestling in prayer for you, that you may stand firm in all the will of God, mature and fully assured.

Eph 4:14-15
Then we will no longer be infants, tossed back and forth by the waves, and blown here and there by every wind of teaching and by the cunning and craftiness of men in their deceitful scheming. Instead, speaking the truth in love, we will in all things grow up into him who is the Head, that is, Christ.

Covenant:
We walk by faith, not alone but within a covenant community. We have joined a salvation throng marching across centuries in conversation with God.

In the beginning God called Abraham and Sarah to be a pilgrim people, to bring blessing to the world (Genesis 12:1-3). The covenant had signs: land, descendants, circumcision, Sabbath. Later, with Moses, the covenant meant deliverance, law, and Liturgy. Always the covenant meant promise and hope.

Obedience is the heart of human response. Biblical covenant is no mere contract. God calls an obedient people. When they disobey, everything falls apart. Isaiah was called to tell this to a people who would not listen – a hard duty (Isaiah 6:1-10). As the forms of sacrifice became superficial, as keeping the law became legalistic, and as religion became ritual without commitment to justice and righteousness, the prophets foretold a new inner covenant. The new covenant would require a circumcised heart.

The sacrifices of God are a broken spirit; a broken and contrite heart,
O God, you will not despise.

Ps 51:17

Jesus Christ, the mediator of a new covenant, has put us right with God and has offered the sacrifice once and for all (Hebrews 9:15-28). Now as a covenant people, we live in promise: "For here we have no lasting city, but we are looking for the city that is to come" (Hebrews 13:14). That city is the new Jerusalem where God and the covenant people will dwell together (Revelation 21:1-6). The Holy Communion is the common meal the covenant people eat together, remembering and waiting (1 Corinthians 11:23-26).

FIVE HABITS

1. Study of God's Word
John 8:31
To the Jews who had believed him, Jesus said, "If you hold to my teaching, you are really my disciples. Then you will know the truth, and the truth will set you free."

2. Prayer
John 14:7-8
If you really knew me, you would know my Father as well. From now on, you do know him and have seen him."
Philip said, "Lord, show us the Father and that will be enough for us."

3. Daily Time with God
1 Cor 1:9
God, who has called you into fellowship with his Son Jesus Christ our Lord, is faithful.

4. Tithing and Service
Deut 4:23
Be careful not to forget the covenant of the LORD your God that he made with you; do not make for yourselves an idol in the form of anything the LORD your God has forbidden.

5. Fellowship and Worship
John 13:34-35

"A new command I give you: Love one another. As I have loved you, so you must love one another. By this all men will know that you are my disciples, if you love one another."

PART F
DISCOVERING HOW GOD HAS SHAPED ME FOR MINISTRY

PERSONAL PROFILE[6]

Name _____ *Year* _____

Spiritual Gifts

Heartbeat

---

[6]Categories drawn from Rick Warren, The Purpose Driven Life: What on Earth Am I Here For, Zondervan, Grand Rapids, 2012, pp.239-246.

Abilities

Personality

Experiences

INTENTIONAL DISCIPLESHIP

One of the biggest challenges in shifting any culture is none other than people. If it weren't for people, everything would be fine. We are a people, a people of God the Father, Jesus Christ, and the Holy Spirit.

The expectations of church members have atrophied over time, leading to frustrations by pastors and dedicated Christian servants. Referring to Kay Kotan's remarks[7] about The United Methodist Church:

"When we moved away from the class meetings and bands that held us accountable for growing more Christ-like, for continuing on our journey, true discipling then began to suffer."

Kay also said:

"We asked them to attend worship, throw a buck in the plate and take care of the building."

Many churches have no intentional discipleship process. As a result, we have generations of people who are not disciples.

There are two key thoughts about nurturing spiritual growth. The first is expectations. The second is intentional discipleship growth.

Expectations

Thom S. Rainer has one of the clearest descriptions of expectations in his book *I am a Church Member*[8]. It would supplement each denomination's specific membership requirements with these six elements:

---

[7]Episode 51 podcast at Lewis Center for Church Leadership, www.churchleadership.com, Kay Kotan and Doug Powe, March 18, 2020

[8]*I am a Church Member* by Thom S. Rainer, B&H Publishing, Nashville, TN, 2013

1. I Will Be a Functioning Member. This is not a membership in a club. I will give, I will serve, I will minister, I will share my story, I will study, I will seek to be a blessing to others. In other words, I will be a kingdom builder, not a kingdom dweller.

2. I Will Seek to be a Source of Unity in the Church. I am not perfect. I will not be a source of gossip or dissension. I will use the Gospel to seek unity of purpose and deed.

3. I Will not let the Church be about My Preferences and Desires. I am in this church to serve Christ and to serve others. I can deal with any inconveniences and matters that are just not my preference or style.

4. I Will Pray for my Pastor Every Day. My pastor must possess more skills than any CEO. His/her work is never done with constant demands for their time. He/she does not have the power to do everything that our church demands. See membership element #1.

5. I Will Lead my Family to be Ambassadors of Christ and Good Church Members. We will pray together for our pastor and our church. We will worship together. We will serve together. We will grow together in the Word.

6. Membership in Christ's Community is a Gift. I received the free gift of salvation. I am humbled and honored to serve and love others in our church and surrounding community. I pray that I will never take my membership for granted and see it as an opportunity to be a part of something bigger than myself or any one person.

I am a church member. Thank God that I am.

PRACTICING DISCIPLESHIP GROWTH

Let's deal with myths and reality.

Myth: Spiritual growth is automatic.
Reality: Spiritual growth is intentional

Myth: Spiritual growth is mystical
Reality: Spiritual growth is very practical (1 Tim. 4:7)

Myth: Spiritual maturity can occur if you find the right "key".
Reality: Spiritual maturity is a process that takes time.

Myth: Spiritual maturity is measured by what you know.
Reality: Spiritual maturity is demonstrated more by behavior than by words.

Myth: Spiritual growth is personal and a private matter.
Reality: Christians need relationships to grow.

Myth: All you need is studying the Bible to grow.
Reality: It takes a variety of spiritual experiences with God to produce spiritual maturity.

Myth: Programs make disciples.
Reality: People make disciples.

If discipleship growth is to be intentional, there needs to be a roadmap. There are many options available on the internet. This is one suggested roadmap.

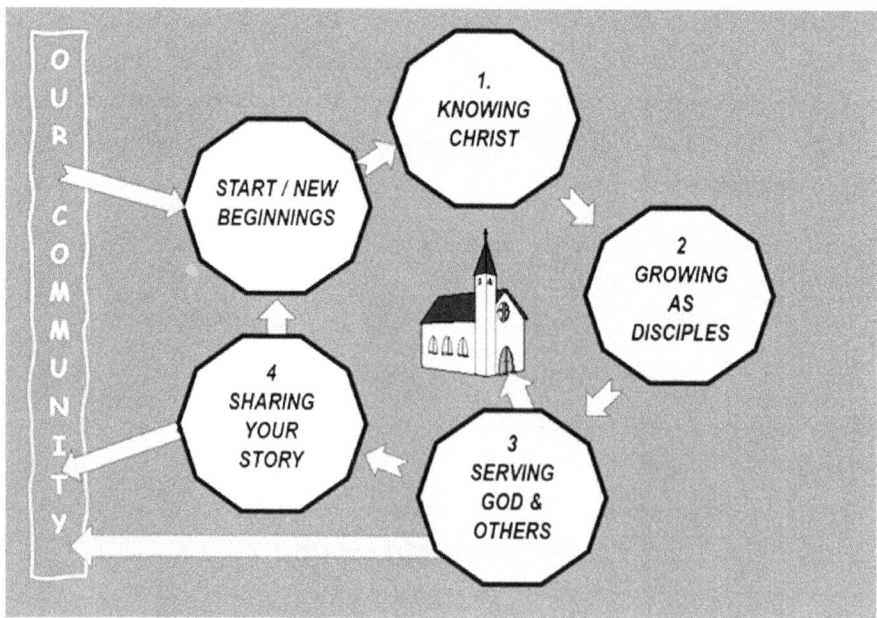

1. Start / New Beginnings
- Introduction to Jesus Christ
- Why You Here on this Earth and Why You Matter
- Basics of the Christian Faith
  - Salvation through Jesus Christ
  - Trinity – Father, Son and Holy Spirit
  - Worship and its rituals
  - Prayer
  - Service
  - Church Seasons
- Orientation to the Bible

2. Knowing Christ
- Doctrine (three graces, baptism, communion)
- Membership Expectations
- Worship (it's a verb)
- Connecting to a Christian Community (small groups, life groups, etc.)

3. Growing as Disciples
- Principles of Spiritual Growth
- Habits for Growth
- Small Group matures as Fellowship / Bible Study / Accountability & Prayer
- Daily Prayer
- Learning to Read and Study the Bible daily.

4. Serving God and Others
- Understanding your Spiritual Gifts
- Discovering your Ministry(ies)
- Serving the Community
- Serving the Local Church
- Facilitating a life group or small group

5. Sharing your Story
- Understanding how Your Life Has Changed
- Understanding how You Have Influenced Others
- Writing Your Story
- Learning How to Tell Your Story

COVENANTS

Each local church ministry should have a covenant with its local church council. Covenants are useful in several ways:

- They give freedom to ministries, so the ministries do not need to come to the church Council for simple decisions. Through this, they create ownership within the ministry and lead to more rapid implementation.

- They provide the ability for the church Council to link activities to the purpose and identity of the church.

- They are a useful tool for transition from one ministry leader to the next.

- They allow/force the church Council to operate at a more strategic level, guiding the direction of the church toward its vision and mission.

Covenants should have:

- Purpose
- Scope
- Goals
- Principles (statements that guide thoughts and actions)
- Objectives for the Coming Year
- Measures of Success

Example Covenant
DEVELOPING DISCIPLES' COVENANT

Mission

Provide a variety of opportunities in Sunday School, Wednesday Night Fellowship Education, Bible studies and retreats that promote and encourage people to develop spiritually during their entire lifetime. Jesus said, "Go therefore and make disciples of all nations, baptizing them in the name of the Father and of the Son and of the Holy Spirit, and teaching them to obey everything that I have commanded you. And remember, I am with you always, to the end of the age." (Matthew 28:19-20)

Scope

Do not be conformed to this world, but be transformed by the renewing of your minds, so that you may discern what is the will of God – what is good and acceptable and perfect. (Romans 12:2)

- Children, youth, and adult spiritual development on Sunday morning.
- Children, youth, and adult spiritual development on Wednesday evenings.
- Adult Bible study, spiritual discernment, and theological reflection/study.
- Confirmation.
- Library as a source of development materials, including books, tapes, and videos.

Principles

- Spiritual development is intentional and comes from God.
- Spiritual growth is a process that is ongoing throughout your life.
- Christians need relationships to grow.
- It takes a variety of spiritual experiences with God to produce spiritual maturity.
- Spiritual maturity is demonstrated more by behaviors than by beliefs.

Objectives

a) Continue two-service Sunday School offering.

b) Expand Vacation Bible School in the number for attendance. We hope to include more from the community.

c) Continue to have educational opportunities throughout summer.

d) Identify leaders for and initiate more in-home Bible studies.

e) Continue to offer leadership courses to teachers twice per year.

f) Evaluate offerings and identify potential opportunities.

g) Draft a schedule of adult educational offerings for the months September to May.

Measures of Success

- 10% increase over the year in youth and children Sunday school attendance. We will continue to keep records of the Sunday School attendance and report to the Council monthly.

- 20% increase over the year in adult attendance on Wednesday evenings. We will begin recording attendance for Wednesday evenings.

- 10% increase in the number of educational small group offerings for adults.

Means to Accomplish

- Develop our offerings based on the Scriptures.

- Model our offerings to include knowledge of the Scriptures and Christian perspective.

- Align our offerings with God's values and character.

- Use the skills God has given us.

- Consider and evaluate the value of having a workshop to evaluate and select specific offerings for adult Christian education.

- Seek outside assistance where appropriate.

> **Committees and Ministry Teams have the following covenant with the Executive Council of the Church and within the Team**

Responsibilities to the Church

- Pray for the Holy Spirit to guide us in our work.

- Seek input on and weigh the impact of our decisions on other ministries, the congregation, the community and the corporate Church.

- Weigh the impact of decisions both short term and long term.

- Recognize that the journey is often as equally important as the results. Spiritual growth is a process.

- Test the organization/team's work at appropriate stages.

- Do everything with enthusiasm; it's contagious.

Responsibilities to Each Other

- Create a safe, collaborative environment with appropriate levels of cooperation and assertiveness.

- Encourage one another with Christian kindness and love.

- Help each other be right – not wrong.

- Look for ways to make new ideas work instead of reasons they won't.

- Forgive each other when we fall short, despite good intentions.

- Celebrate each other and everyone's spiritual gifts.

Decision Making

- Clarify the decision to be made. Make sure everyone has the same understanding.

- Know the timeframe for making the decision. Understand the risks of missing the time window and not making a decision.

- Strive for consensus* in place of voting**.

- Be guided by Church vision, Church direction, and audience/benefactor of the outcome as issues and possible solutions are discussed.

Communication

- Communications from the team will be drafted, reviewed by the team and upgraded, if necessary, before release.

- Periodically test whether the messages are being received and understood.

- Be concise in communications.

- Respond to requests and input. Be prompt, consistent with other guidelines.

Listening and Feedback

- Seek first to understand.

- Communicate openly, honestly and tactfully.

- Seek input from organization/team and from people impacted by the direction, objectives and decisions.

Attendance
- Attend all meetings or send a substitute.
- If unable to attend a meeting, the individual takes responsibility to determine what occurred at the meeting.
- Attend meetings that occur on short-term notice on a best-efforts basis.

Confidentiality
- Except for personnel items within staff personnel committee, meeting business should be public.
- Personal items shared within a meeting should remain confidential.

Meeting Design and Leadership
- Meetings should be designed to address the most critical items and make best use of the participants' time.
- Meeting minutes should be kept for the team and published within xx days of the meeting.

* Consensus means that everyone understands the decision and can explain why it is best; everyone can live with the decision. The decision is not necessarily everyone's top choice; no one opposes it. Consensus is not a unanimous vote or a majority vote. It requires time, active participation of all group members, skills in listening, conflict resolution and discussion facilitation, and creative thinking and open-mindedness.

** Voting can be used:
- When consensus is highly unlikely within the time allowed.
- When members are equally informed on the subject matter and understand one another's viewpoints.
- When it is determined that the majority can handle the implementation without the active involvement of those who vote "no"

CHAPTER 3
FOCUSING ON PURPOSE AND IDENTITY

Laity empowerment and congregational transformation does not occur with more training, more involvement in activities, or pulpit exhortations. It always begins with a renewed focus on purpose and identity for both individual believers, each ministry and committee, and the congregation as a whole.

We have found there are three important questions to answer. Churches that address them and are able to answer are far more likely to thrive than those who do not.

The first critical question is: "What is our purpose?"
Answering this question begins with discerning what God is calling the congregation to do, not what we as individuals or as a church board think should be our purpose. The result comes not from a brainstorming session where everyone offers their ideas and then the group seeks consensus around what may be regarded as best. Instead, a process of discernment, involving Bible study and prayer, leads to discovery of what God is calling the congregation to do.

There is often confusion about the differences between vision, mission, and purpose. This can lead to many wasted hours of "word-smithing". We have chosen Purpose & Identity for clarity in thought and action at the individual level, the ministry level and the church level.

This image of the church life cycle can be very helpful in discerning where your church is today:[9]

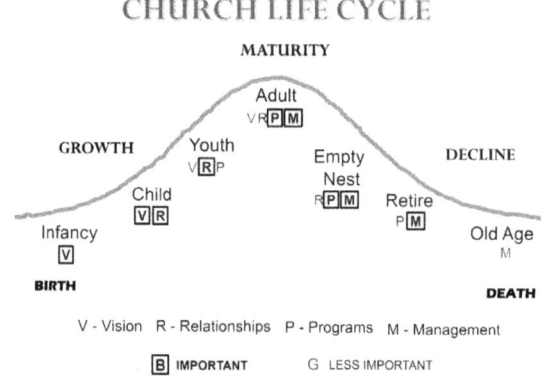

Like every living organism, a congregation is born, grows to maturity and, without appropriate intervention, dies. The difference between our physical bodies and the church, though, is that churches can be renewed and begin a new life cycle if the focus is on purpose & identity and the appropriate changes made.

Bishop Bob Farr, of the Missouri Annual Conference of the United Methodist Church, likens purpose to driving his beloved 1966 Mustang. In the tight "cockpit" there is room for only one driver to guide the car. Multiple drivers would not get the vehicle to its intended destination and could, conceivably, result in an accident that injures those inside the car as well as others.[10] The very same result can occur in a congregation that is trying to function with multiple, often conflicting, purposes.

---

[9] Brighton Passages, adapted from George Bullard, Congregational Passages: *The Life Cycle and Stages of Congregational Development, New Reformation Solutions*, 1999

[10] Healthy Church Workshop, Baltimore Washington Conference, 2013

In the early days of a church the purpose, or "driver", is clearly the vision that led to the congregation's birth. Everything that happens is devoted to carrying out that vision. The focus is definitely outward as members seek to share their vision with others whom they hope will want to join them.

As the congregation grows, however, relationships become more important. As such, they seek to move into the driver's seat. Members enjoy being together in a common effort and tend to resent and resist anything that may cause relationships to suffer. At its fullest expression this can lead to folks saying things like, "We can't do that because it will hurt Bill's feelings," or "Before we do that, we need to make sure everyone approves of the idea." Relationships are certainly important, but not to the extent where they might detract from the primary focus on purpose.

The next stage in a congregational life cycle occurs when programs become central. To some extent, this is a function of growth in numbers that requires more activities to involve as many as possible. Of course, adding programs requires additional staff and more resources to support the multiple activities. Not uncommonly, this results in multiple committees and groups each pursuing their own purpose rather than working together toward the common congregational purpose. Think, if you will, of a football field where multiple members of a team are vying for position. The result is lots of activity but very little movement toward the goal.

As people grow tired of so much activity and fall away, decline often begins to occur. With dwindling resources of people and money, the focus shifts to maintenance and survival. Paying the bills and keeping the doors of the church open is what drives virtually every decision being made. For most churches, this represents a death spiral from which there is little chance of recovery.

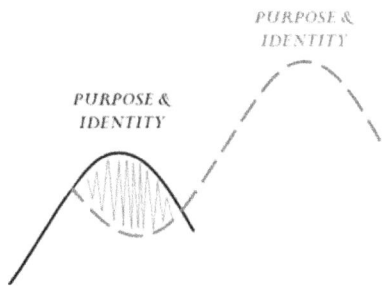

The important thing to remember, though, is that a new life cycle can be started at any point on the curve in the diagram. Admittedly, this is much easier to accomplish while the congregation is still growing toward maturity. Once the downward curve begins, renewal is much more difficult, if not impossible. All of this makes it essential for the church to accurately identify where they are in the life cycle (their identity) and then take steps (best done with a skilled coach or consultant) toward revitalization and new life.

We have found, over and over again, that every new life cycle for a congregation involves a renewed focus on purpose and identity. Especially now, in the current climate of chaos and uncertainty, it is imperative for congregations to fully understand and commit to a renewed sense of purpose. Decisions regarding human and material resources are all made in light of how they will enable the church to achieve its God-given purpose. This is the driver that leads to vital ministry.

The second question is: "Who are we?"
This is the question of identity. Finding the answer is not as easy as it may sound. For it is not a matter of who we have been, what we would like to be, or who we might become. Rather, this step requires an objective and honest appraisal of who the congregation is right now.

The process is not unlike going for one's annual physical. We would like the doctor to say everything is fine. But if there are problems present, it is essential to diagnose and treat them. Surprisingly, many people avoid going to the doctor precisely because they don't want to know if anything is wrong with their body. And many congregations resist such an honest self-assessment for much the same reason. It's easier by far to just assume, or pretend, that everything is just fine, no matter the long-term cost.

The problem with this approach is that it presents a false picture of the congregation and provides a shaky foundation for any efforts toward growth and vitality. We have seen many change efforts fail simply because they begin at the wrong place with an inaccurate picture of the church's identity. Later in this chapter we will provide a tool to help you accurately and honestly assess your congregation's true identity.

The third question is "Who are our neighbors?"
Purpose and Identity have little meaning without context. We must ask who our neighbors are and know the community in which we pray, worship, and serve. Answering these questions helps clarify the context:

- Where do people live, work and play?

- What are the demographics? Singles, families, or retired? Transient or stable?

- What is the culture of the community?

- What is the spiritual maturity – unchurched vs. churched, perception of faith communities?

No church can be all things to all people. Effective congregations tailor their purpose to the distinctive needs of the community in which they are planted. The landscape is littered with empty churches that failed to do just that, preferring instead to do what they've always done because it is most comfortable even though the community around them has changed dramatically. What works in one context may not work in another.

There is another way to think about this question.

Is our church visible in the community? Is it playing a vital role? Would local citizens know the name of our church and what it does in the community?

Discerning Your Church's Current Purpose & Identity
To understand your current purpose & identity:
1. Discuss where your church is on the life cycle framework and why.
2. What type of church are you? What are your values?

Types and Values of American Churches[11]

Type of Church	Unifying Value	Role of Pastor	Role of People	Primary Purpose	Typical Tool	Desired Result
Classroom Church	Doctrine	Teacher	Students	To Know	Sermon Outline	Educated Christians
Soul-winning Church	Evangelism	Evangelist	Bringers	To Save	Altar Call	Born-again Christians
Experiential Church	Worship	Worship Leader	Worshipers	To Exalt	Liturgy	Devoted Christians
Family Church	Fellowship	Chaplain	Care & Support	To Belong	Social Activities	Secure Christians
Disciple Building Church	Personal Growth over lifetime	Guide & Shepherd	Personal Study & Prayer	To Grow	Small Groups	Committed Christians
Ministry Church	Service	Outward Focus	Aiding Others	To Serve	Outreach Programs	Visible Christians

Your church will have all of these types to certain degrees. Some values will be more dominant than others. See the next chapter for ways to process this as a team.

Developing a Revised / Upgraded Church Purpose Statement

Some things to keep in mind as the congregation works to discern and develop a purpose statement. An effective purpose statement is 1) Biblical, 2) Specific, and 3) Measurable. Church consultant Bill Easum emphasizes that a church's purpose statement should be simple enough that it can be memorized by any first-grade child.[12] We've been in churches where we've seen purpose statements posted on walls or bulletin boards that are several pages long. That is not an effective purpose statement. Even multiple paragraphs represent too much verbiage. Some examples of effective purpose statements might be:

---

[11] modified and improved from pg 44 of *Look before you Lead* by Aubrey Malphurs, Baker Books, Grand Rapids, Michigan, 2013

[12] Exponential Conference, Orlando, FL, 2013

- Experience the Love of Jesus and Give it Away
- Praising God, Growing Disciples, and Serving the World
- God's Family Pursuing God's Kingdom
- Reach Up, Reach Out, and Reach In
- Revive Believers, Reach Friends, and Renew Culture
- Be Used by God to Change Lives, Strengthen Churches, and Transform the World
- Know Jesus and Make Jesus Known

Once the congregational purpose is discerned it becomes vital to keep it in front of everyone so there is no doubt about what the church is called to do, and the purpose becomes a living document. Purpose statements like those above are succinct enough to be printed on everything: letterhead, web page, worship bulletin, monthly newsletter, etc. The purpose should be repeated at the beginning of every church meeting and event so everyone understands clearly why they have come together. And those who answer the phone (or the automated message after hours) can repeat the statement. "This is Second Church where our purpose (or mission) is to experience the love of Jesus and give it away," how can I help you?

It is important to open every worship service with a repetition of the purpose. As the worship leader offers a welcome it might go something like this, "Welcome to First Church, where our purpose (or mission) is to praise God, grow disciples and serve the world." You will know the purpose has been successfully implanted when the congregation answers back or repeats the statement along with the worship leader!

And when it comes time for the offering, the pastor or worship leader can give examples of how the purpose is being accomplished and made possible as a result of the congregation's giving.

Making the Purpose Alive in Each Ministry and Each Person

Purpose should cascade throughout the organization. Each ministry should have a purpose, expressed as a covenant. And each member should have a personal purpose that reflects the Holy Spirit in their heart and the gifts that God has given them (see Chapter 2). All these (sub) purposes should be aligned to the Great Commission and the Great Commandment. It is the responsibility of the highest administrative body of the church to test and assure that alignment.

Each local church ministry should have a covenant with its local church council. Covenants are useful in several ways:
- they give freedom to ministries, so the ministries do not need to come to the church Council for simple decisions; thereby creating ownership within the ministry that leads to more rapid implementation.
- they provide the ability for the church Council to link activities to the purpose and identity of the church
- they are a useful tool for transition from one ministry leader to the next
- they allow/force the church Council to operate at a more strategic level, guiding the direction of the church toward its vision and mission.

Covenants should have:
- Purpose
- Scope
- Goals
- Principles (statements that guide thoughts and actions)
- Objectives for the Coming Year
- Measures of Success

Example covenants are in Chapter 2.

Finally, each person should have an individual purpose statement that reflects what God has equipped them to do and what God has shown that person to do. Remember:
- You were planned for God's pleasure.
- You were formed for God's family.
- You were created to become like Christ.
- You were shaped for serving.
- You were made for a PURPOSE.[13]

Rick Warren, in his book "The Purpose Driven Life – What on Earth am I Here For?" cites:

> *It's in Christ that we find out who we are and what we are living for. Long before we first heard of Christ and got our hopes up, he had his eye on us, had designs on us for glorious living, part of the overall purpose he is working out in everything and everyone.*
>
> **Ephesians 1:11-12 MSG**

So, a very big step toward partnering for vital ministry involves asking and answering these three questions: 1) What is our purpose? 2) Who are we? and

---

[13] These are the chapter headings in Rick Warren, The Purpose Driven Life, Zondervan, Grand Rapids, 2012.

3) What is the context in which God has placed us? Biblical verses to aid in discerning church and personal purposes can be found in the tools section of this chapter.

LIVE IT OUT

- Consider initiating a church-wide Bible study focused on God's purpose for the church.

- Create or upgrade your church purpose in a way that seeks God's will for your faith community. Involve key leaders as described in Chapter 3 to build insight and commitment to the purpose.

- Organize a group to honestly assess where your congregation is in the Life Cycle of a Church.

- Establish a covenant, which includes a purpose, for each ministry.

- Provide the means for each member to create a personal life purpose. Create a group to understand your community, perhaps using the tools of Mission Insite.[14]

- Listen to these podcasts at The Lewis Center for Church Leadership, Wesley Theological Seminary (www.churchleadership.com)

- Podcast Episode 4 "Becoming an Outward-Focused Church" featuring Junius Dotson

- Podcast Episode 46 – "How Can Churches Thrive in a Time of Cultural and Institutional Change?" featuring David McAllister-Wilson

- Engage a team of leaders to work through the three exercises in this chapter

- Evaluate what mental models guide your own and the congregation's ministries.

---

[14] Mission Insite reveals insights about the community around you, so you can move from data to decisions, www,missioninsite.com.

CHAPTER 3
FOCUSING ON PURPOSE AND IDENTITY
✸ TOOLS

Purpose & Identity are critical to changing church culture – at the church level, at the ministry/committee level and at the individual level. Some tools to help are:
- Additional Biblical Verses about Purpose
- "What is Church" Exercise
- Church Purpose Exercise
- Personal Purpose Exercise

The prayer and scripture are offered for spiritual grounding as you use these tools.

PRAYER

Holy God, you have created and called everyone to love you and neighbors. But so often, the busyness of our lives and our own cares and concerns crowd out our commitment to fulfilling your purpose. Help each of us and the congregation to engage in prayer and study so that we might better discern your purpose for our life together. Clear away the competing priorities of our days and lead us to re-commit to loving you and others in your name. Amen.

SCRIPTURE

"Teacher, which is the greatest commandment in the Law?"

Jesus replied: "'Love the Lord your God with all your heart and with all your soul and with all your mind.' This is the first and greatest commandment. And the second is like it: 'Love your neighbor as yourself.' All the Law and the Prophets hang on these two commandments."

Matt 22:36-40

"You are the salt of the earth. But if the salt loses its saltiness, how can it be made salty again? It is no longer good for anything, except to be thrown out and trampled underfoot.

"You are the light of the world. A town built on a hill cannot be hidden. Neither do people light a lamp and put it under a bowl. Instead they put it on its stand, and it gives light to everyone in the house. In the same way, let your light shine before others, that they may see your good deeds and glorify your Father in heaven.

Matt 5:13-16

ADDITIONAL VERSES FOR STUDY AS YOU CONSIDER YOUR CHURCH PURPOSE AND YOUR PERSONAL PURPOSE

Matt 25:34-40

"Then the King will say to those on his right, 'Come, you who are blessed by my Father; take your inheritance, the kingdom prepared for you since the creation of the world. For I was hungry and you gave me something to eat, I was thirsty and you gave me something to drink, I was a stranger and you invited me in, I needed clothes and you clothed me, I was sick and you looked after me, I was in prison and you came to visit me.'

"Then the righteous will answer him, 'Lord, when did we see you hungry and feed you, or thirsty and give you something to drink? When did we see you a stranger and invite you in, or needing clothes and clothe you? When did we see you sick or in prison and go to visit you?'

"The King will reply, 'Truly I tell you, whatever you did for one of the least of these brothers and sisters of mine, you did for me.'

Matt 28:18-20

Then Jesus came to them and said, "All authority in heaven and on earth has been given to me. Therefore go and make disciples of all nations, baptizing them in the name of the Father and of the Son and of the Holy Spirit, and teaching them to obey everything I have commanded you. And surely I am with you always, to the very end of the age."

Mark 10:43-45

Not so with you. Instead, whoever wants to become great among you must be your servant, and whoever wants to be first must be slave of all. For even the Son of Man did not come to be served, but to serve, and to give his life as a ransom for many."

Luke 4:18-19

"The Spirit of the Lord is on me, because he has anointed me to proclaim good news to the poor. He has sent me to proclaim freedom for the prisoners and recovery of sight for the blind, to set the oppressed free, to proclaim the year of the Lord's favor."

John 13:34-35

"A new command I give you: Love one another. As I have loved you, so you must love one another. By this everyone will know that you are my disciples, if you love one another."

John 20:21

Again Jesus said, "Peace be with you! As the Father has sent me, I am sending you."

Acts 1:8

But you will receive power when the Holy Spirit comes on you; and you will be my witnesses in Jerusalem, and in all Judea and Samaria, and to the ends of the earth."

Acts 2:41-47

Those who accepted his message were baptized, and about three thousand were added to their number that day.
They devoted themselves to the apostles' teaching and to fellowship, to the breaking of bread and to prayer. Everyone was filled with awe at the many wonders and signs performed by the apostles. All the believers were together and had everything in common. They sold property and possessions to give to anyone who had need. Every day they continued to meet together in the temple courts. They broke bread in their homes and ate together with glad and sincere hearts, praising God and enjoying the favor of all the people. And the Lord added to their number daily those who were being saved.

Acts 4:32-35

All the believers were one in heart and mind. No one claimed that any of their possessions was their own, but they shared everything they had. With great power the apostles continued to testify to the resurrection of the Lord Jesus. And God's grace was so powerfully at work in them all that there were no needy persons among them. For from time to time those who owned land or houses sold them, brought the money from the sales and put it at the apostles' feet, and it was distributed to anyone who had need.

Rom 15:1-7

We who are strong ought to bear with the failings of the weak and not to please ourselves. Each of us should please our neighbors for their good, to build them up. For even Christ did not please himself but, as it is written: "The insults of those who insult you have fallen on me." For everything that was written in the past was written to teach us, so that through the endurance taught in the Scriptures and the encouragement they provide we might have hope.

May the God who gives endurance and encouragement give you the same attitude of mind toward each other that Christ Jesus had, so that with one mind and one voice you may glorify the God and Father of our Lord Jesus Christ.

Accept one another, then, just as Christ accepted you, in order to bring praise to God.

Gal 5:13-15

You, my brothers and sisters, were called to be free. But do not use your freedom to indulge the flesh; rather, serve one another humbly in love. For the entire law is fulfilled in keeping this one command: "Love your neighbor as yourself." If you bite and devour each other, watch out or you will be destroyed by each other.

Gal 6:1-2

Brothers and sisters, if someone is caught in a sin, you who live by the Spirit should restore that person gently. But watch yourselves, or you also may be tempted. Carry each other's burdens, and in this way you will fulfill the law of Christ.

Eph 2:19-22

Consequently, you are no longer foreigners and strangers, but fellow citizens with God's people and also members of his household, built on the foundation of the apostles and prophets, with Christ Jesus himself as the chief cornerstone. In him the whole building is joined together and rises to become a holy temple in the Lord. And in him you too are being built together to become a dwelling in which God lives by his Spirit.

Eph 3:14-21

For this reason I kneel before the Father, from whom every family in heaven and on earth derives its name. I pray that out of his glorious riches he may strengthen you with power through his Spirit in your inner being, so that Christ may dwell in your hearts through faith. And I pray that you, being rooted and established in love, may have power, together with all the Lord's holy people, to grasp how wide and long and high and deep is the love of Christ, and to know this love that surpasses knowledge—that you may be filled to the measure of all the fullness of God.

Col 1:24-28

Now I rejoice in what I am suffering for you, and I fill up in my flesh what is still lacking in regard to Christ's afflictions, for the sake of his body, which is the church. I have become its servant by the commission God gave me to present to you the word of God in its fullness—the mystery that has been kept hidden for ages and generations, but is now disclosed to the Lord's people. To them God has chosen to make known among the Gentiles the glorious riches of this mystery, which is Christ in you, the hope of glory. He is the one we proclaim, admonishing and teaching everyone with all wisdom, so that we may present everyone fully mature in Christ.

Col 3:15-17

Let the peace of Christ rule in your hearts, since as members of one body you were called to peace. And be thankful. Let the message of Christ dwell among you richly as you teach and admonish one another with all wisdom through psalms, hymns, and songs from the Spirit, singing to God with gratitude in your hearts. And whatever you do, whether in word or deed, do it all in the name of the

Heb 10:24-25

And let us consider how we may spur one another on toward love and good deeds, not giving up meeting together, as some are in the habit of doing, but encouraging one another—and all the more as you see the Day approaching.

1 Peter 2:9-10

But you are a chosen people, a royal priesthood, a holy nation, God's special possession, that you may declare the praises of him who called you out of darkness into his wonderful light. Once you were not a people, but now you are the people of God; once you had not received mercy, but now you have received mercy.

1 John 1:5-7

This is the message we have heard from him and declare to you: God is light; in him there is no darkness at all. If we claim to have fellowship with him and yet walk in the darkness, we lie and do not live out the truth. But if we walk in the light, as he is in the light, we have fellowship with one another, and the blood of Jesus, his Son, purifies us from all sin.

1 John 4:7-21

Dear friends, let us love one another, for love comes from God. Everyone who loves has been born of God and knows God. Whoever does not love does not know God, because God is love. This is how God showed his love among us: He sent his one and only Son into the world that we might live through him. This is love: not that we loved God, but that he loved us and sent his Son as an atoning sacrifice for our sins. Dear friends, since God so loved us, we also ought to love one another. No one has ever seen God; but if we love one another, God lives in us and his love is made complete in us.

WHAT IS CHURCH?[15] EXERCISE

What are the essentials of church? Decide as a group which things you will cross off as non-essential and which things you will circle as essential. It may help to consider the question using this thought process: If we didn't have _____ could we still have church? Feel free to write in the blanks anything you consider essential that is missing from the list.

Sanctuary	Sunday School	Youth Ministry
Jesus	Coffee	God
Worship Service	Holy Spirit	VBS
Children's Ministry	Choir	Bible
Music	Potluck Dinners	Baptism
Prayer	Preacher	Mission
Women's Ministry	Communion	Hospitality
Bible Study	Evangelism	Fellowship
Softball Team	Outreach	Committees
Organ	Money	Worship Bane
Book of Common Worship	Book of Discipline	Offering
Hymnal	Nursery	Mission Trips

---

[15] Michael Beck, New Room Conference, 2019

CHURCH PURPOSE EXERCISE

A. *Why does our church exist?*

B. *How are we unique? What do we offer that no other "organization" can?*

C. *What are we to **be** as a church?*

D. *What are we to **do** as a church?*

PERSONAL PURPOSE EXERCISE

A. Why do I exist?

B. How am I unique? What do I offer that no one else can?

*C. As a disciple of Christ, what am I called to **be**?*

*D. As a disciple of Christ, what am I to **do**?*

CHAPTER 4
DISCERNING CULTURE

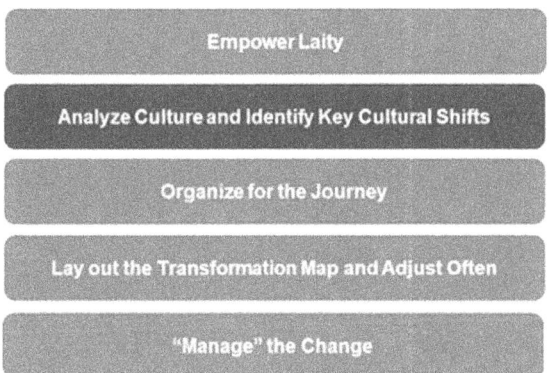

Discerning purpose, identity, and context, and involving laity in ministry are essential steps. But these are not yet a sufficient base from which to launch strategies for change. The next, and in many ways most crucial, step is to discern your congregation's culture. Leadership Consultant Samuel Chand says that "culture—not vision or strategy—is the most powerful factor in any organization."[16]

---

[16]*Cracking Your Church's Culture Code* by Samuel R. Chand, Jossey-Bass, San Francisco, CA, 2011

We have found this observation to be incredibly important. In our journey as dean and coach with the first two Financial Leadership Academies, we discovered that new and/or better practices alone did not create vitality and generosity. Even with the best of intentions and equipped with excellent strategies, many of our pastors failed to effect lasting change, because their attempts occurred in what could only be described as a culture that was not open to change.

Improvement in and sustainment of vitality and generosity required a shift in local church culture. As Dick Clark claimed in an issue of "Executive Leadership," *"The fact is, culture eats strategy for lunch. You can have a good strategy in place, but if you don't have the culture and the enabling systems, the (negative) culture of the organization will defeat the strategy."* [17] Based on our experiences with many churches we would go further and say that *culture eats strategy for breakfast, lunch, and dinner!*

But what is culture?
Culture is an expression of values. It is tradition (like in Fiddler on the Roof). It resides in the hearts and minds of people. Culture is the UNWRITTEN pattern of responses discovered, developed or invented during a group's history of handling problems. The responses, reinforced through time, are considered the correct way to perceive, feel, think and act. They are passed on to new members through immersion and teaching.

Each of us create patterns (also known as mental models) to deal with the complexity of the world as well as to fit in (and be liked) by the group we are a part of. A culture is a way of life of a group of people--the behaviors, beliefs, values, and symbols that they accept, generally without thinking about them, and that are passed along by communication and imitation from one generation to the next.[18] Culture is the shared set of assumptions, values, and beliefs of a group of people by which they organize their common life.[19]

---

[17] Dick Clark quoted in "Corporate Culture Is the Game," Executive Leadership, Nov. 2008, 3.

[18] http://people.tamu.edu/~i-choudhury//culture.html

[19] Wederspahn, Gary, Intercultural Services (Managing Cultural Differences), Houston: Gulf Publishing, 2000

According to Gil Rendle, *"Culture will reflect what is rewarded/recognized. People will do what they are paid to do (staff) or given recognition (laity), not what they are asked to do!"* [20]

Many people do not recognize culture and/or its importance. They are immersed in it. They can't see the forest for the trees. Many wish to change their church but feel overwhelmed, asking questions like where do I start, how do I lead, do I direct or encourage, how do I deal with resistance, etc.? In this chapter and the next, we will discuss how to think about culture and how to pursue one that is more desirable.

Whose culture are we talking about?
- Personal (know thyself)
- Group cultures (music, trustees, Sunday School, etc.)
- Local church
- Community
- Denomination

There is no formula or recipe for dealing with culture. Every church's culture is different. Likewise, the need to exegete observe and interpret it. The means to redirect or change the culture will differ from church to church and it will have many dimensions. We will give you a transformation map to see and manage those dimensions.

The change in culture will be NON-LINEAR. It will be, at times, discomforting. For some it will feel chaotic. Through it all, your leadership will need to be SPIRITUAL, helping God's people take the next faithful step and disturbing your church and culture in the right direction.

We should pause and say that we are not proposing changing the entire culture. Parts of the culture are beneficial in that they reinforce the values that the church

---

[20] Rendle, Gil, *Waiting for God's New Thing: Spiritual and Organizational Leadership in the In-Between Time,* www.thf-fdn.org, Texas Methodist Foundation, April 2015

wishes to sustain on its journey. Therefore, it is important to discern all the elements of culture and choose which to reinforce and which to change.

One of the benefits and challenges of Andy's 31-year pastorate at Glen Mar Church was the opportunity to live through multiple congregational culture shifts. When he arrived in 1979, Glen Mar was a small country chapel celebrating 25 years of ministry since its founding by pioneers who were mostly farmers and merchants.

The congregation had remained small, even though the new community of Columbia, MD, was growing rapidly around it—built on acres of farmland purchased by the Rouse Corporation with the intent of creating a prototypical city of the future. As might be imagined, there was great resentment by long-time county residents—including Glen Mar members—toward their new neighbors. Therefore, the first culture shift required overcoming that resentment in order to reach out in mission to residents of the new community.

The resulting congregational growth created the need for a second culture shift, from a small to medium sized church. In a small church, everyone knew everyone else. The pastor (Andy) knew everyone's name and could drive to their home without aid of maps or directories. The first resistance came with the creation of a second worship service. This may sound familiar to many of you! At the same time, additional staff became necessary, thus expanding the web of relationships and further distancing many from direct contact with the pastor.

Growth continued at a dramatic pace, making Glen Mar the fastest growing United Methodist church in its conference (Baltimore Washington) during the 1980's. A third worship service was added in order to provide for the hundreds of people coming through the front door each Sunday. At the same time, it quickly became apparent that large numbers were also exiting through the back door. Out of a desire to grow, the congregation had unwittingly focused on an attractional ministry. The next culture shift, then, was to move toward a discipling ministry so that people came not just for the "show" but to be equipped to serve.

For those who stayed through this phase (and many chose to find other churches) the required shift was from spectators to active participants in ministry. A 3-year period of intense congregational Bible study and strategic planning led to wide-ranging reorganization of structure and "the way we do things here." Virtually all standing committees were abolished in favor of ministry teams who planned, executed and evaluated specific ministries (often without the pastor's knowledge). The congregation adopted a mantra of "Blessed to be a Blessing," in which every individual was seen as gifted and called by God to serve.

This commitment to serve led the congregation to the next culture shift—the decision to leave a fully paid, beautiful sanctuary and organ to move to a new 21-acre campus from which they could better serve the needs of the community. The congregation now worships in a space that functions as a gym during the week. They then exit the property past a sign that reads "Exit to Serve" as they go from worship into the world.

We'll have more to say about the challenges and costs of these culture shifts in later chapters. But, it can accurately be said they were not painless, resulted in loss of members and constituted the hardest work Andy as pastor and the congregation ever did. They were also an experience that drove home the need for culture to change in order for growth and vitality to occur.

Representing Culture as an Iceberg

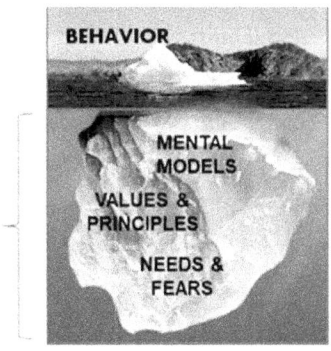

We will discuss culture as Mindsets & Behavior. Behavior is the manifestation of culture – what we see (what's above the water). What drives Behavior are Mindsets – what we can't see (what's below the water).

Behavior is reactive, ego-centric, or purposeful.[21]

- Reactive behavior is a response to an external stimulus.

This can be positive or negative. Procedures and standard ways of doing tasks tap the reactive behavior. They are used for those inexperienced in the task, to ensure consistency of outcome and to enhance productivity.

It can be positive in response to danger.

Generally, a negative reactive behavior is grounded in the ego.

- Ego-centric is the internal drive to be better than others.

One of the major shifts in society is from affiliation to individuality. In many circumstances, institutions which proliferated during the twentieth century became untrustworthy or did not live up to their creeds. The loss of value in affiliation drove people to make decisions in their own self-interest.

This egocentricity by an individual within an organization is behind their hidden agendas and passive/aggressive behavior.

- Purposeful refers to the identity and values that are more than self, working to serve something greater.

This behavior brings the alignment of divergent views. The overall purpose and identity of an organization must be translated into team/committee purpose and individual purpose in order for intentional behavior to be internalized and sustained.

Slow down your mental processes to self-observe behavior while working or in a particular situation. This is only possible in purposeful behavior. Self-observing is seeing and interpreting your behavior and trying to improve it in the moment. Self-remembering is an audit of what was done and creating the means to do better the next time.

Mindsets are created from needs and fears, values, principles, and mental models.

---

[21]Charles G. Krone & Associates, organizational effectiveness consulting with E.I. DuPont de Nemours, 1981

- Needs and Fears are physiological, safety, belonging, and esteem requirements; the bottom two-thirds of Maslow's hierarchy. [22]
- Values are standards derived from our beliefs.

But the fruit of the Spirit is love, joy, peace, patience, kindness, goodness, faithfulness, gentleness and self-control. Against such things there is no law.
Galatians 5:22-23 NIV

Jerry Hurley, of Life.Church observes that: "If I can't remember a time it cost me something, then it isn't a core value. The number one force that shapes your culture is your values."[23]

- Principles are comprehensive guidance to guide values into actions. Craig Groeschel describes his church's principles (which he calls values)[24]:

    - **We will honor Christ and His church with integrity.** If we live with integrity, nothing else matters. If we don't live with integrity, nothing else matters.

    - **We will do anything short of sin to reach people who don't know Christ.** To reach people no one is reaching, we'll have to do things no one is doing.

    - **We always bring our best.** Excellence honors God and inspires people.

    - **We give up things we love for things we love even more.** It's an honor to sacrifice for Christ and His church.

    - **We are spiritual contributors not spiritual consumers.** The church does not exist for us. We are the church and we exist for the world.

    - **We are faith-filled, big thinking, bet-the-farm risk takers.** We'll never insult God with small thinking and safe living.

---

[22]https://en.wikipedia.org/wiki/Maslow%27s_hierarchy_of_needs
[23]Craig Groeschel Leadership Podcast # 67, Building a Strong Culture: Q&A with Jerry Hurley
[24]IBID

- **We will lead the way with irrational generosity.** We truly believe it is more blessed to give than to receive.

- **We are all about the "capital C" Church.** The local church is the hope of the world and we know we can accomplish infinitely more together than apart.

- **We will laugh hard, loud and often.** Nothing is more fun than serving God with people you love.

- **We wholeheartedly reject the label mega-church.** We are a micro-church with a mega-vision.

• Mental models are internal images, assumptions, and patterns of how the world works; they also guide our actions. Jay Wright Forrester in 1971 stated, "The image of the world around us, which we carry in our head, is just a model. Nobody in his head imagines all the world, government, or country. He has only selected concepts, and relationships between them, and uses those to represent the real system."[25]

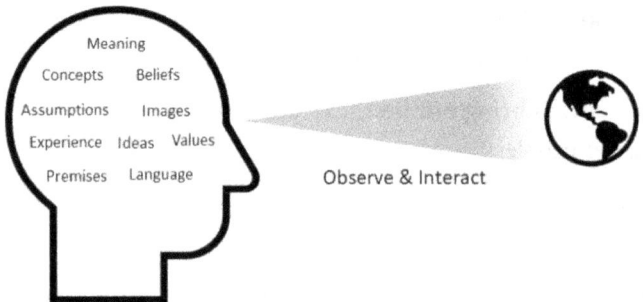

Characteristics of a mental model are that they are:
- Founded on incomplete facts.
- Constantly evolving, in inverse proportion to age.
- An information filter – causes selective perception, perception of only selected parts of information.
- Very limited, compared to the complexities of the world.

---

[25]https://quotefancy.com/jay-wright-forrester-quotes 1971

Many people are unaware they use mental models. They may say, "Based on my experience…" or "My thought processes led me to conclude…"

Peter Senge stated, "Mental models are deeply held internal images of how the world works; images that limit us to familiar ways of thinking and acting. Very often, we are not consciously aware of our mental models or the effects they have on our behavior."[26]

All models are wrong, but some models are useful. In the world of mental models, every person has unique mental models. This concept is useful in being a leader and reconciling differences. The dilemma is not who is right (that is, whose mental model is right). Instead, the challenge is to use tools to understand and make visible the basic assumptions and values that underlie the perspectives.

What do you value?

There are several means to understanding yourself, which is the first step to being a great leader. Prepare to be surprised if you create an atmosphere of safety with the people you ask. Ted did this with feedback on a 360-degree evaluation of his performance in one of his business roles. The feedback from his direct reports differed significantly from the feedback received by his peers and senior leaders. When he asked his direct reports for details, he was shocked, downcast and sad. He was told that he was role playing (not being authentic) and that he was so rigid he mistook the edge of the rut for the horizon. But the feedback for Ted was a gut-check that changed his demeanor and business value system for the better.

Different ways to receive feedback include:
- Ask your spouse and/or family
- Ask your accountability group
- Play The Values Deck, similar to the card game Ted used in his business experience.

---

[26]Senge, Peter M., The Fifth Discipline: The Art & Practice of the Learning Organization, pg. 174, Doubleday, New York, New York, 1990

- Consult "How to Define Your Personal Values and Live by Them for a Fulfilling Life" by Evelyn Marinoff[27] that provides a values audit
- Utilize Myers-Briggs type indicator test

Other means to discern your culture include:
- Folklore (stories that people frequently tell that indicate what is important)
- Rituals (the pattern of how things are done; e.g. meetings)
- Norms (styles of deference, dress codes)
- Taboos (things that are admonished)
- Success Symbols (what is lifted up in communications, meetings and worship announcements)
- Governance (how problems are solved and decisions made)
- Organization (structure communicates relative importance)
- Financial Priorities (what is core and what can be deferred)

Let's close out this chapter on Discerning Culture by looking at some statements.
- Strategy is intentional. Culture is habit.
- Culture is the environment in which your strategy and brand thrives, or dies.
- Culture either drives or drains people's energy and motivation.
- "Culture isn't just one aspect of the game, it is the game." Lou Gertner, former CEO at IBM.
- People are loyal to the culture, not to strategy.
- Culture may provide resilience in tough times.
- Culture is your brand, your differentiator among faith communities. God as the Trinity is the brand in the secular world.

LIVE IT OUT

- Identify and assess your current culture.

---

[27] https://www.lifehack.org/866227/personal-values

CHAPTER 4
DISCERNING CULTURE TOOLS

The tools include:
- **Practices Survey***
- **Church Type/Church Values***

The prayer and scripture are offered for spiritual grounding as you use these tools.

PRAYER

Loving God, we are far too willing to see the best in ourselves while condemning what we perceive as the shortcomings of others. Help us to see ourselves clearly and objectively so that we might begin the work of transformation that will make of us better followers of The Way. Lead us to pursue your will for us, both individually and as a congregation. In Jesus' name, Amen.

---

* A PDF version of this tool can be requested at www.changingchurchculture.com

SCRIPTURE

"Why do you look at the speck of sawdust in your brother's eye and pay no attention to the plank in your own eye? How can you say to your brother, 'Let me take the speck out of your eye,' when all the time there is a plank in your own eye? You hypocrite, first take the plank out of your own eye, and then you will see clearly to remove the speck from your brother's eye."

Matthew 7:3-5

The following two exercises are designed to first create individual assessment of your church and then create a shared assessment of your church.

EXERCISE 1 - PRACTICES SURVEY

1.) Each person in the leadership team should complete the following table individually.

For each pair of statements (A and B), please indicate which one more closely describes your congregation by circling any one of the five numbers in the middle column.

Circling **1** says that statement **A** best describes your church.

Circling **5** says that statement **B** best describes your church.

Circling **2** says that statement **A** somewhat betters describes your church.

Circling **4** says that statement **B** somewhat betters describes your church.

Circling **3** says that you are unsure or neutral. Please avoid circling 3 as much as you can.

Statement A	Mostly A	More Like A	Neutral	More like B	Mostly B	Statement B
Our members practice their spirituality personally	1	2	3	4	5	Our church practices its spirituality corporately
Our church is separate from society	1	2	3	4	5	Our church is integrated with society
Our church values a pastor who delivers great sermons and provides pastoral care	1	2	3	4	5	Our church values a pastor who provides vision and direction
Uncertainty means there are risks to be avoided	1	2	3	4	5	Uncertainty means there are opportunities to be explored
The pastor is expected to shape the direction of the church	1	2	3	4	5	Laity leaders and the pastor jointly shape the direction of the church
We depend on rules and procedures as an essential basis in our decision making	1	2	3	4	5	Rules and procedures function as broad guidelines in our decision making
Our focus is on completing important ministry tasks	1	2	3	4	5	Our focus is on cultivating relationships
We focus on numbers	1	2	3	4	5	We focus on spiritual health and vitality
The majority of the church's ministry is done by a few	1	2	3	4	5	Most members (>50%) understand their gifts and talents and use them in service
Visitors are alone in the crowd	1	2	3	4	5	Visitors feel welcomed
Our focus is only on our church members	1	2	3	4	5	Our focus is balanced internally and externally
We emphasize programs	1	2	3	4	5	We emphasize how programs change lives
Most members use sermons as their primary Biblical insight	1	2	3	4	5	Most members are bible literate and apply its teachings daily
The church's main mission is to take care of its church family	1	2	3	4	5	The church's main mission is to make disciples
We attract visitors who look like members	1	2	3	4	5	We attract people who are different from the majority of the worship attenders

Statement A	Mostly A	More Like A	Neutral	More like B	Mostly B	Statement B
Few members can recite from memory the purpose/mission of the church	1	2	3	4	5	Most members can recite from memory the purpose/mission of the church
Most attendees see themselves as members	1	2	3	4	5	Most attendees see themselves as ambassadors for Christ
Most members plateau after joining the church	1	2	3	4	5	Our church has a clear pathway for growimng as disciples and members know where they are on the path
The Sunday sermon provides the main Bible study for most members	1	2	3	4	5	More than 50% of worship attendees are in small groups for fellowship, growth in Biblical literacy, and prayer
Our church is invisible in the community	1	2	3	4	5	Our church is well known in the community and considered vital to its success

2.) Choose someone to compile the results, showing range and average for each of the twenty topics.

3.) There are no wrong observations. Rather, discuss the differences in perception.

4.) Does the composite reflect your church? How should it change to reflect God's calling for your church?

5.) This helps you discern the current culture and identify the elements of your desired culture.

EXERCISE 2 - CHURCH TYPE / CHURCH VALUES

What values do you infer from your church's type? Ask your leaders to rank individually. Have someone compile the results and use the compilation to generate discussion about the current state and the future state that God sees for your church.

Rating 6-Highest 1-Lowest	Type of Church	Unifying Value	Role of Pastor	Role of People	Primary Purpose	Typical Tool	Desired Result
	Classroom Church	Doctrine	Teacher	Students	To Know	Sermon Outline	Educated Christians
	Soul-winning Church	Evangelism	Evangelist	Bringers	To Save	Altar Call	Born-again Christians
	Experiential Church	Worship	Worship Leader	Worshipers	To Exalt	Liturgy	Devoted Christians
	Family Church	Fellowship	Chaplain	Care & Support	To Belong	Social Activities	Secure Christians
	Disciple Building Church	Personal Growth over lifetime	Guide & Shepherd	Personal Study & Prayer	To Grow	Small Groups	Committed Christians
	Ministry Church	Service	Outward Focus	Aiding Others	To Serve	Outreach Programs	Visible Christians

1.) Individually rate each description of values from 1 – highest to 6 – lowest for your church. Use the descriptors to aid you in your analysis. Use each number only once.

2.) Choose someone to compile the results, showing range and average for each type of church. Each church will be multiple types but usually two or three dominate.

3.) There are no wrong observations. Rather, discuss the differences in perception.

4.) Does the composite reflect your church? How should it change to reflect God's calling for your church?

5.) This also helps you discern the current culture and prioritize the values of your desired culture.

CHAPTER 5
SHIFTING CULTURE

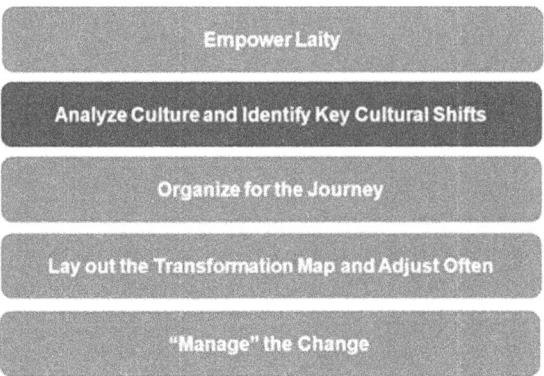

Now that you have a clear view of your existing culture and a future desired culture, the question becomes: What shifts do I/we need to make?

- What Personal shifts are important for pastors and laity leaders?
    - What are my values?
    - Can I "see" my mindsets and behavior?

- Where are my loyalties?
- What am I willing to sacrifice in order to lead culture shift?
- Can I use a resource like "The Purpose Driven Life" to guide my personal shift?

• What shifts in team and church culture are important in moving towards our Purpose & Identity? Keep in mind that an effective purpose is 1) Biblical, 2) Specific, and 3) Measurable. The desired shifts should move the church in directions that meet these criteria.

One church catalogued their shifts as:

Focus on Numbers	→	Focus on Spiritual Health & Vitality
Nurturing by a Few	→	Each person is being nurtured and each person cares for others
Majority of work done by a few	→	Majority of members understand their gifts and talents and utilize them in service
Event-oriented mindset for missions	→	Every day provides an opportunity for every Person to do missional service
Visitors are alone in the crowd	→	Visitors feel that they belong
Children and youth ministries are outdated	→	Core message is the same; the medium of delivery is relevant to today.
Giving does not support the budget	→	Giving supports operating budget and provides for new opportunities to serve.
Internal Focus	→	Internal and external balance
Pastor led	→	Laity and pastor led
Fragmented communications	→	Intergrated communications with clear contacts for answers
Emphasis on activities	→	Emphasis on how activities change lives

Some of these shifts may seem minor. But others represent major change. Bishop Bob Farr, in Renovate or Die[28], points out that many churches are more inclined to make only minor changes that resemble re-decorating or changing appearance when renovation is really needed.

Renovation begins by making sure the foundation is in order, the structural walls are in good shape, the roof is solid, and the carpenters have the right tools and materials for the job. Renovating is much more aggressive than redecorating. It is more in depth and has greater personal cost....Renovating is a long process and is expensive.[29]

Throughout this process, Farr says that mission (purpose in our terms) is the plumb line for change. "You must measure everything by whether or not it is achieving the mission."

It is important at this stage to create a vision for yourself and your congregation. This vision summarizes the purpose, identity and culture shifts you and your team wish to make. Later in this chapter, you will find tools to create a vision that:

- **creates a common intention**
  As a result, there is a feeling of unit in the network/community. There is also a feeling of empowerment. Individuals know where the church is headed and do not have to keep checking with the pastor or council chair.

- **aligns the total person**
  Everything the person does is related to achieving the vision. For example, athletes do visualization exercises, seeing themselves doing it right a hundred times. The effort required to achieve the goal is then imprinted on the athlete's mind.

---

[28] Renovate or Die – 10 Ways to Focus Your Church on Mission by Bob Farr with Kay Kotan, Abingdon Press, Nashville, TN, 2011

[29] IBID, 8

- **stimulates awareness**

It sensitizes people to the issue and helps them make the vision a reality. For example, if the vision relates to attracting "seekers", people are suddenly more aware of how "seekers" may see traditional churches and what changes are necessary.

- **inspires people and draws them in**

People feel as if they are a part of an important effort.

Organize for the Journey

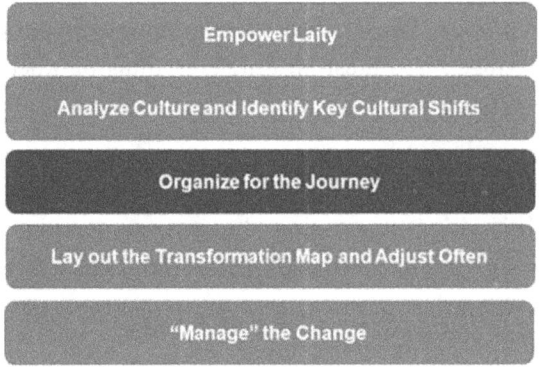

The next step is to organize for the journey.
What it will feel like when you try to make the change by yourself:

To avoid these feelings, create a network of leaders from both structural positions and from the congregation as a whole.

This network will:
- Be influence leaders from the congregation
- Be influence agents in positional authority
- Be a sounding board and test kitchen for ideas and implementation tactics.
- Maintain a cadence of accountability for all transformation work.

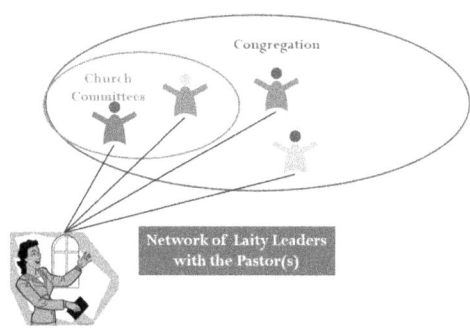

Characteristics of these leaders:

- Recognize that commitment to Jesus Christ is the foundation for all leadership.
- Future oriented.
- Seek to respond to conflict as Jesus did – directly, openly and responsibly.
- Earnestly seek God's will for the church. They work diligently, work with tenacity, and they respect the view of others to bring about the changes that are needed.
- Determined to be servant-leaders, seeking the good of the kingdom rather than their own power and status.

Paul Nixon, in "I Refuse to Lead a Dying Church," advises pastors to "keep a list of the bright-eyed people, the people who are energized by the thought of their church living and thriving in ministry."[30]

---

[30] Paul Nixon, I Refuse To Lead a Dying Church, Cleveland, The Pilgrim Press, 2006, 32.

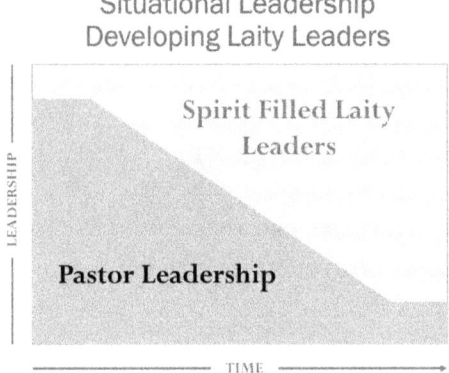

In most cases but not all, the pastor provides the majority of leadership during the initial phases of the effort. Through time, these leadership responsibilities are transferred to laity leaders as they develop understanding of their roles and leading skills.

Lay out the Transformation Map and Adjust Often

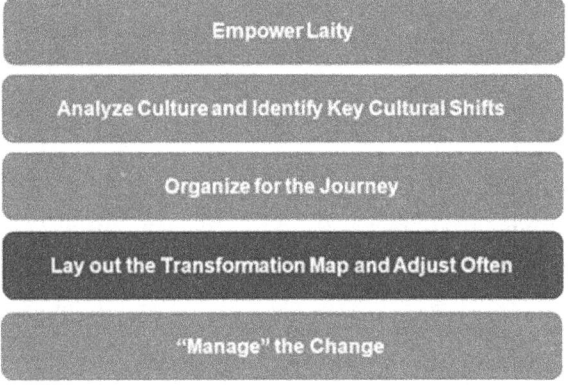

Now we know where we want to go (vision), why we want to go (purpose & identity) and have recruited a team to plan the journey. When we travel by car, we usually have a roadmap, either on a piece of paper or digitally. In the case of cultural change, we may try to copy another church. BUT that would be a mistake! We need to create a map that recognizes the uniqueness of our church and what God is calling us to do.

So, how do we do this?
  • Create a multi-year Transformation Map by a ministry/committee of the church.*

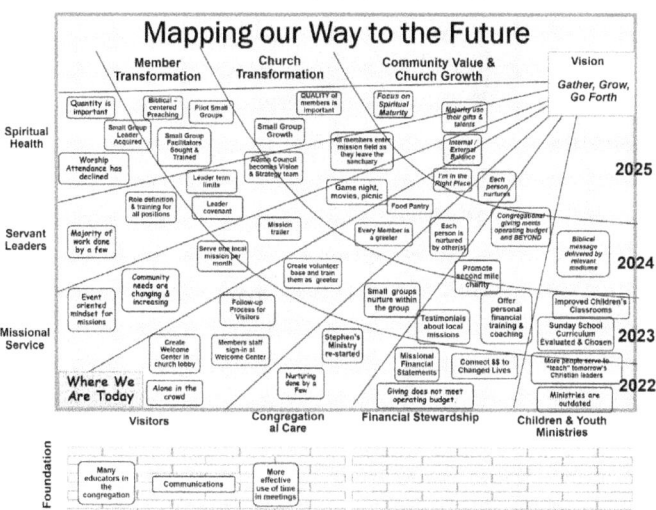

See full image on next page

The Transformation Map[31] is an integrated set of actions to achieve God's will for your church. The map itself:

- Communicates the Purpose & Identity and "journey" to the entire congregation.
- Builds momentum and focuses energy toward common goals and aligning ministry teams
- Identifies conflicting initiatives and interdependencies across ministries and committees, making everyone better able to see what others are doing and the implications that may have
- Better manages chaos by anticipating future change
- Improves our ability to set priorities and request service
- Improves the ability to identify barriers to achieving goals and develop an action plan

---
* A PDF version of this tool can be requested at www.changingchurchculture.com
[31] Adapted from *Supply Chain Transformation Mapping 040427*, Capgemini, 2004

118 • Empowering Leaders

Shifting Culture • 119

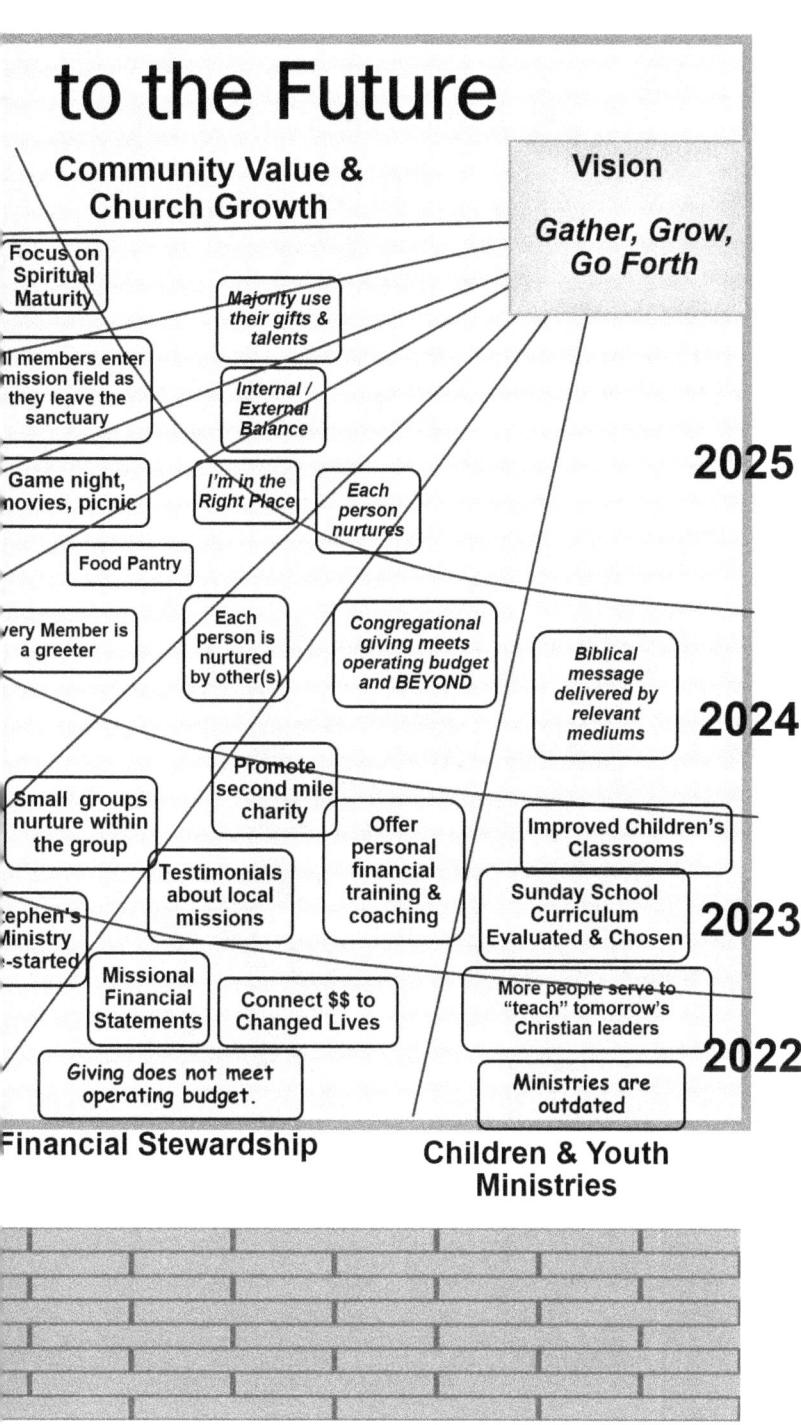

- Identifies implementation plans that must be developed and identify the milestones
- Provides the ability to track progress towards the desired state described by Purpose & Identity.

The process for creating a transformation map is described later in this chapter.
- Utilize Project Management for each implementation plan.
  - Basic project management is described in the tool section of this chapter.
  - 4DX is an excellent tool.[32]
  - Utilize SMART goals (specific, measurable, achievable, realistic, timely)
- Be directionally correct and adjust frequently. This becomes the responsibility of the Executive Team of the church after sufficient alignment and buy-in occurs.

"Manage" the Change

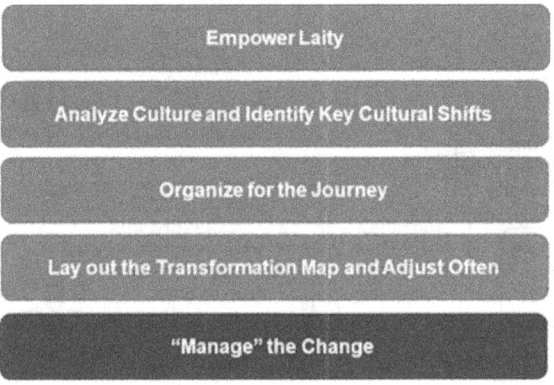

Manage is put in quotations because it does not mean control the change, as some may do. It really means lead the change, much of which we will discuss in subsequent chapters.

---

[32]Chris McChesney, Sean Covey, Jim Huling, The 4 Disciplines of Execution, New York, Free Press, 2012.

- Use creative tension; adjust the zone of disequilibrium.

Too little tension creates no change. Too much tension alienates even the most ardent supporters of the change. The system is like a pressure cooker: set the temperature and pressure too low, and you stand no chance of transforming the ingredients. Set the pressure and temperature too high and the cover will blow off.

The Productive Zone of Disequilibrium

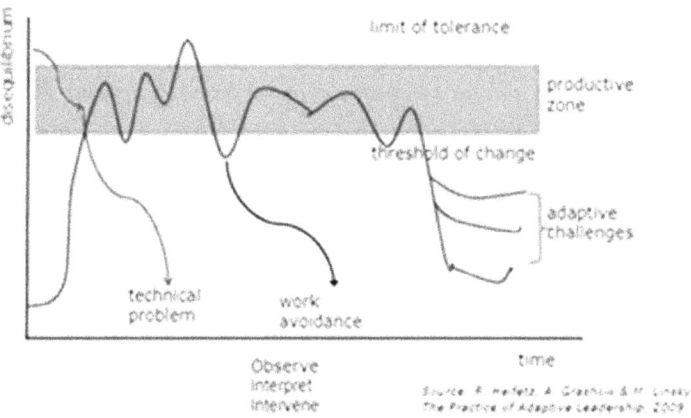

Joe Ellis in Adaptive Leadership in Organizations, Future Proofing your Culture, OnTrack International, November 2015, gives some techniques for increasing heat into the system and for decreasing heat in the system. These are summarized in the tools section of this chapter.

- Use the balcony to see what's happening on the dance floor.

Ronald Heifetz and Marty Linsky , authors of the best-selling Leadership on the Line (Harvard Business Review Press, 2017) stated in 2002:

> *Leadership is an improvisational art. You may be guided by an overarching vision, clear values, and a strategic plan, but what you actually do from moment to moment cannot be scripted. You must respond*

as events unfold. To use our metaphor, you have to move back and forth from the balcony to the dance floor, over and over again throughout the days, weeks, months, and years. While today's plan may make sense now, tomorrow you'll discover the unanticipated effects of today's actions and have to adjust accordingly. Sustaining good leadership, then, requires first and foremost the capacity to see what is happening to you and your initiative as it is happening and to understand how today's turns in the road will affect tomorrow's plans.

But taking a balcony perspective is extremely tough to do when you're fiercely engaged down below, being pushed and pulled by the events and people around you—and doing some pushing and pulling of your own. Even if you are able to break away, the practice of stepping back and seeing the big picture is complicated by several factors. For example, when you get some distance, you still must accurately interpret what you see and hear. This is easier said than done. In an attempt to avoid difficult change, people will naturally, even unconsciously, defend their habits and ways of thinking. As you seek input from a broad range of people, you'll constantly need to be aware of these hidden agendas. You'll also need to observe your own actions; seeing yourself objectively as you look down from the balcony is perhaps the hardest task of all. Fortunately, you can be both an observer and a participant at the same time.[33]

- Respect others' ideas, concerns and fears. Use one of the many tools described later in the chapter.
- Acknowledge the loss of comfort (a value for many) and the possible fear of the unknown.
- Accept failure.
- Accept Loss.
- Apply your Purpose to Everything

---

[33]Heifetz, Ronald & Linsky, Marty, *A Survival Guide for Leaders*, Harvard Business Review (magazine), June 2002

In Chapter 8 of The Purpose Driven Church, Rick Warren states:

"Now we come to the most difficult part of becoming a purpose-driven church. Many churches have defined their purposes and developed a purpose statement; they regularly communicate their purposes to their membership; some have even reorganized their structure around their purposes. However, a purpose-driven church must go one step further and rigorously apply its purposes to every part of the church: programming, scheduling, budgeting, staffing, preaching, and so forth.

• Integrating your purposes into every area and aspect of your church's life is the most difficult phase of becoming a purpose-driven church. Making the leap from a purpose statement to purpose-driven actions requires leadership that is totally committed to the process. The application of your purposes will require months, maybe even years, of praying, planning, preparing, and experimenting. Take it slow. Focus on progress, not perfection."[34]

• Use Cultural Guides to Lead Others

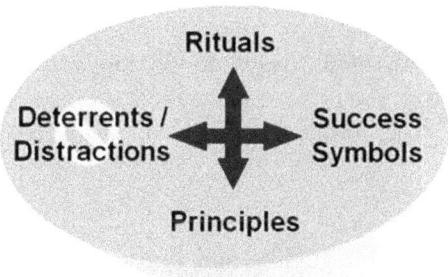

When you lead a transformation, some people will be faithful followers without understanding the where, what and why of the change. Cultural guides act as signs and guardrails to help you throughout the journey.

---

[34] Warren, Rick, The Purpose Driven Church: Growth without Compromising your Message & Mission, Zondervan, 1995, pg. 137

✓ Rituals

- Rituals systematically remind people of the change that is desired. The worship service is a ritual. The facilities and how they are used are a ritual that reflects culture.

- Rituals can include organization structure and church council agendas.

✓ Success Symbols

- Acknowledgment and publicity of the achievement of key milestones.

- Without acknowledgment, the effort put forth may be "just good enough".

✓ Deterrents and Distractions

- Some actions reinforce the old culture. These need to be addressed in a respectful way and not permitted to detract from the desired cultural change.

- Unknown paradigms (ways of looking at something) silently restrain people.

✓ Principles

An effective tool for guiding and developing others is the use of principles. A principle can be defined as a moral rule or belief that helps you know what is right and wrong and that influences your actions. Principles are designed to guide actions and depart from asking for permission for everything that is done.

An example is "Worship is a verb". This provides guidance about the worship service. We assemble to worship God. If the music is for the performers to shine or to entertain the congregation, then we are not following the principle. If the sermon is to edify understanding but leads to no action, then worship has become a Sunday School lesson. If worship primarily becomes a social gathering (as revealed by energy and time committed to gathering), then the primary purpose of adoring God is lost. If worship is the convenient time to corner the pastor about some issue or concern instead of facilitating their preparation for worship, then we are diverting the pastor's thoughts from prayerful greetings.

Other principles may be:
- The Church Council's business is God and enacts the strategy to live out Purpose & Identity.
- We will test everything against our Purpose & Identity.
- We will be honest in all communications and be as transparent as possible.
- We will warmly greet all types of people who enter our church and treat them with respect.

You can craft a principle statement for every shift in culture you wish to make.

Harry L. Reeder III's book From Embers to a Flame, How God Can Revitalize Your Church is thought provoking and can suggest principles you may want to make for your own church. For example, we may learn from the past without living in the past. Or, we will acknowledge and repent for sins committed against our community.[35]

LIVE IT OUT
- Create a team of leaders to guide the change process.
- Create a principle statement for each culture shift you seek to make
- Implement the last four Stages of Transformation Leadership

---

[35] Reeder III, Harry L., *From Embers to a Flame: How God Can Revitalize Your Church*, Phillipsburg, New Jersey, P&R Publishing, 2008

CHAPTER 5
SHIFTING CULTURE

Shifting the culture is hard and it takes persistence and stamina. These tools will help make the shift:
- Shaping a Vision
- Culture Shift Exercise
- Transformation Mapping
- Change Readiness and Progress Checklist
- Executing the Transformation Map/Getting Things Done
    - Getting Things Done
        - Meetings
        - Guidelines for Effective Decisions
        - Project Management
        - Clarifying Roles - RACI
    - Improving the Work of the Church

The prayer and scripture are offered for spiritual grounding as you use these tools.

PRAYER

Eternal Father, you have created us in your image and called us to reconcile the whole world to you. We acknowledge how far short we have fallen. Many of our words and actions fail to reflect your image in a way that helps others know you better. Much of our life together reflects exclusiveness, suspicion and mistrust rather than the love you have called us to share. Forgive us for our shortcomings and inspire us to forge a new beginning, both as individuals and as a congregation, so that we might reveal your love and grace in all we do and say. Amen.

SCRIPTURE

Therefore, I urge you, brothers and sisters, in view of God's mercy, to offer your bodies as a living sacrifice, holy and pleasing to God—this is your true and proper worship. Do not conform to the pattern of this world, but be transformed by the renewing of your mind. Then you will be able to test and approve what God's will is—his good, pleasing and perfect will.

For by the grace given me I say to every one of you: Do not think of yourself more highly than you ought, but rather think of yourself with sober judgment, in accordance with the faith God has distributed to each of you. For just as each of us has one body with many members, and these members do not all have the same function, so in Christ we, though many, form one body, and each member belongs to all the others. We have different gifts, according to the grace given to each of us. If your gift is prophesying, then prophesy in accordance with your[a] faith; if it is serving, then serve; if it is teaching, then teach; if it is to encourage, then give encouragement; if it is giving, then give generously; if it is to lead,[b] do it diligently; if it is to show mercy, do it cheerfully.

Romans 12:1-8)

Therefore, if anyone is in Christ, the new creation has come: The old has gone, the new is here! All this is from God, who reconciled us to himself through Christ and gave us the ministry of reconciliation: that God was reconciling the world to himself in Christ, not counting people's sins against them. And he has committed to us the message of reconciliation. We are therefore Christ's ambassadors, as though God were making his appeal through us. We implore you on Christ's behalf: Be reconciled to God. God made him who had no sin to be sin for us, so that in him we might become the righteousness of God.

2 Corinthians 5:17-6:1

SHAPING THE VISION: WHAT IS INVOLVED?*

As leaders begin to shape the vision at various levels, they ask questions such as:

- What kind of church do we want to be?
- What will it be like if we implement our strategy?
- What do we want people to say as a result of our work?
- What values are most important to us?
- How does this vision represent biblical teachings?
- What is the large value of this task?
- What place do I have in this vision of the future?

Regardless of the vision's scale or the level at which it is employed, an very good vision is:

- Clear
- Involving
- Relevant
- Linked to the organization's overall strategy
- Linked to the Great Commission
- Memorable

---

* A PDF version of this tool can be requested at www.changingchurchculture.com

- Meaningful beyond tasks
- Seen as a "stretch" -- difficult but not impossible
- A reflection of group values
- Better than the current situation

There are four different tools for shaping the vision – News Articles, Values, Analogies, and Pictures. The process of using these tools creates dialogue, understanding and alignment among the church leaders. Utilize all the tools to create input for finalizing the vision. (Remember that you can revisit and revise the vision during the transformation journey.)

SHAPING THE VISION: TOOLS

News Article: Vision of the Future

This tool helps you visualize a successful future for your church. Imagine that you are a journalist writing an article for your favorite newspaper or magazine. Create a story that vividly describes your church at a future time. It may be 1, 2, or even 10 years from now. Assume that your church has been very successful.

Hint: When writing your article, include:

- Colorful phrases
- Emotional words
- Clear images
- Customer-oriented goals
- Positive effects on customers and work-group members

Headline: _____

Story: _____

Values of the Church

Think about what you and your church community value most. Then respond to the following statement.

In my church, we really care about:

1. _____

2. _____

3. _____

4. _____

5. _____

Analogies to Shape a Vision

Analogies and metaphors are types of imagery. An analogy describes one thing as if it were something else. We use analogies when we say things such as, "My teenager's room is a pigpen." Or "Our annual budgeting meeting is like a three-ring circus; there's something happening every minute." Metaphors and smiles can be very effective when you are shaping the vision for the church. For example, you might say, "I think of the church as a wood shelter -- open, safe haven, and ready to accept you as you are." Listed below are categories that will prompt you to describe the church using metaphors and similes. For each category, note the image that comes to mind.

"If I were to describe our church community as a (fill in one of the categories below), I would say it is . . ."

Color: Movie:

Season: Machine:

Sport: Emotion:

Geographic Location: Food or benverage:

Song or other music: Other image:

Drawing a Picture of the Future

On a large sheet, draw a picture of the future for the church and its community. What images will illustrate your vision? Use pens, pencils, or colored markers to draw your vision.

SUMMARY: CREATING A VISION WITH YOUR CHURCH

1. The major themes that emerge from my work with the vision tools are:

2. The vision for our church is:

3. Our plans for communicating the vision and involving the congregation are:

CULTURE SHIFT EXERCISE

List the key paradigm shifts to successfully achieve your purpose & identity. This becomes Step 1 of Transformation Mapping

From:	To:

TRANSFORMATION MAPPING

Mapping Is a Tool That Can Help Us Lay More Groundwork for Actionable Change in a Church

Our mapping of the future may include:
- A profile of what the church will look like at a specific time in the future.
- The future "purpose & identity"" picture.
- The church's future organizational picture and characteristics.
- An integrated set of key actions that must be undertaken/in place to realize the new purpose & identity
- The culture (values) and goals that guide the church members.

We can use it to achieve many objectives:
- Communicate vision, identity & purpose, and "journey" to the entire church
- Build momentum and focus energy towards common goals… aligning ministry teams and committees.
- Identify conflicting initiatives and interdependencies across ministries and committees, enabling them to see what others are doing and the implications that may have on us
- Better manage chaos by anticipating future change
Identify barriers to achieving vision and develop an action plan
- Develop implementation plans and identify milestones
- Track progress towards Future State

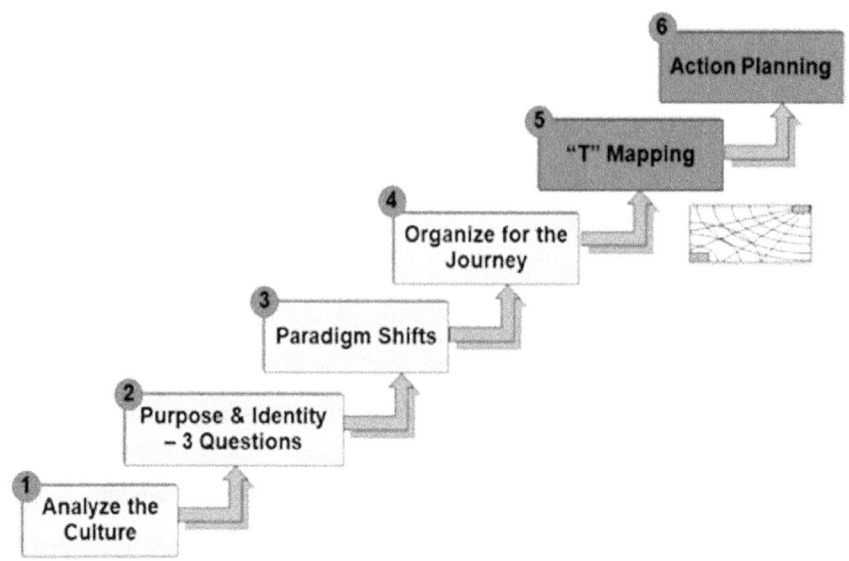

Transformation Mapping helps enroll people in building a blueprint for action while Action Planning translates the game plan into short term actions and objectives for individuals within the Church.

The Transformation Map is a Simple but Powerful Framework to Chart the Changing Profile of a Church

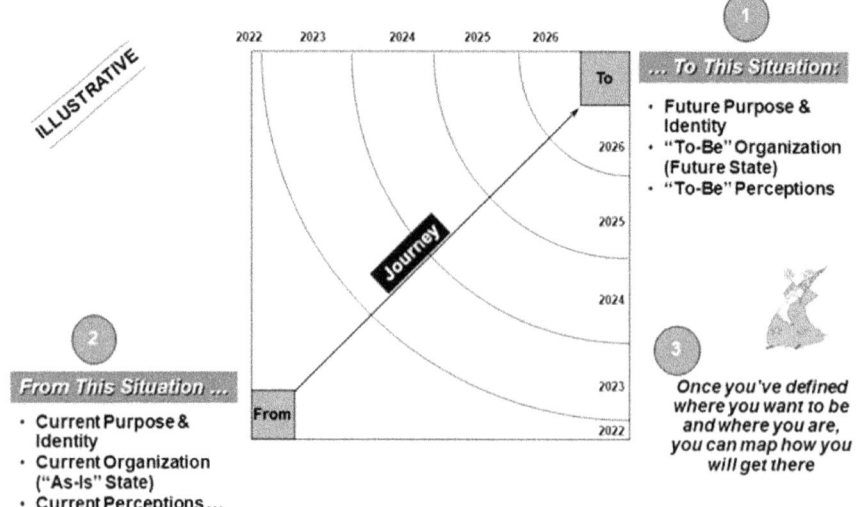

Shifting Culture • 135

Step 1: Our Views on the "To" (Where We Want To Be) & "From" (Current State We Are in Today) for our Church

Based on culture shift exercise, LIST THE TOP FIVE paradigm shifts in culture for your church:

1. _____   1. _____

2. _____   2. _____

3. _____   3. _____

4. _____   4. _____

5. _____   5. _____

Step 2: Choose Categories/Dimensions for a Multi-year Integrated Plan

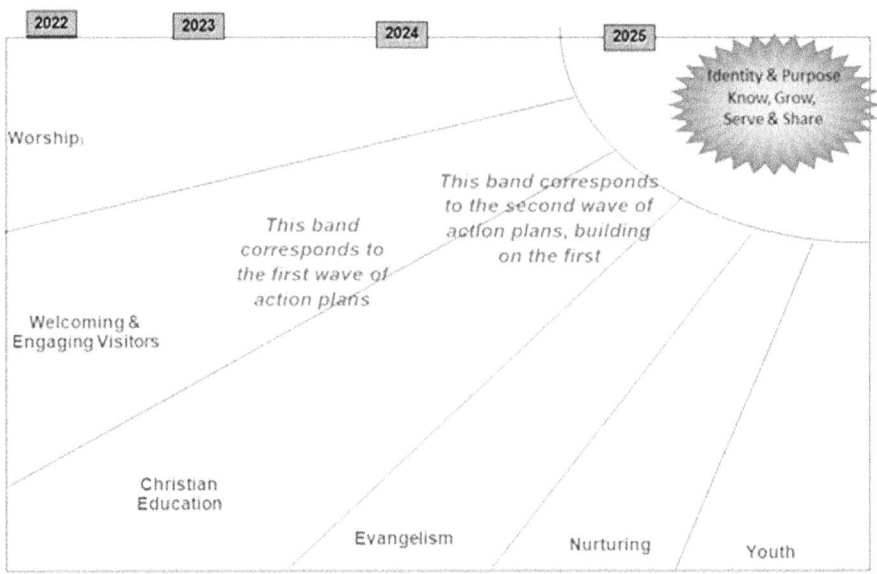

Step 3 Map Our Path of Action Plans Backward From Our Future

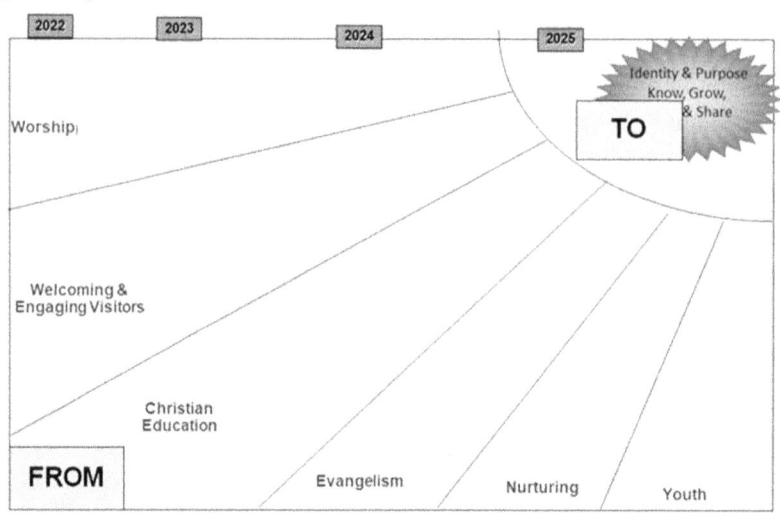

For each category/dimension:

1. Describe (in a few words) your category (ministry/committee) when we get to our desired Purpose & Identity.

2. Define what must be in place to achieve the Purpose & Identity for category (ministry/committee)

3. What are the gaps and barriers to achieving the goal for your category (ministry/committee)?

4. Define "actions" which must be done to eliminate the barriers and close the gaps.
- Resources
- Work Process or Practices
- Roles
- Training

5. Group the actions, if required.

6. Place into a sequence (build backwards from the future to the basics)

7. Synchronize the ministries and committees on goals and timing.

Charter key projects (action plans) to achieve the first and second year objectives.

Example of Transformation Map

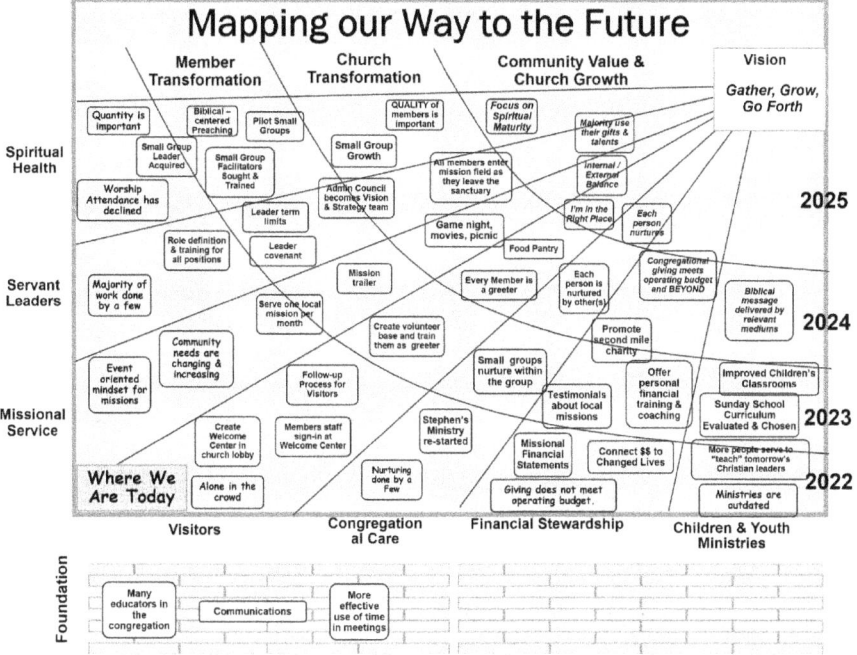

The Value of Transformation Mapping is in the Process as Much as the Outputs*

- Building the Transformation Map is the first step
- Through communication events, the Vision, Purpose, & Identity are shared with all church members
- Feedback is key to building momentum and gaining ownership throughout the church family
- Some churches maintain the Map and update it as part of their strategic planning process

---

* A Powerpoint version of this tool can be requested at www.changingchurchculture.com

CHANGE READINESS & PROGRESS CHECKLIST*

Use this checklist to assess your preparedness for change and to assess progress at key checkpoints.

Name (optional): _____

Church: _____

	Often	Somewhat			Never	
Leading Change	5	4	3	2	1	**Comments**
Information provided by leadership is trusted.						
The leaders embrace a common purpose and identity.						
There is a clear dissatisfaction with the current state in most organization and opinion leaders.						
Plans and guidance are directionally correct during the change process.						
Leaders are visible engaged in the change process.						
Shaping a Vision	5	4	3	2	1	**Comments**
Information provided by leadership is trusted.						
The leaders embrace a common purpose and identity.						
There is a clear dissatisfaction with the current state in most organization and opinion leaders.						
Plans and guidance are directionally correct during the change process.						
Leaders are visible engaged in the change process.						

*A PDF version of this tool can be requested at www.changingchurchculture.com

	Often		Somewhat		Never	
Preparing the Plan	5	4	3	2	1	**Comments**
The plan considers all ministries and committees.						
Leaders are involved in development of the plan.						
The plan to achieve the vision can be done in a relatively short time (2-4 years).						
The plan can be visually communicated in a transformational map						

Creating a Shared View	5	4	3	2	1	**Comments**
The desired state, guided by purpose & identity, has been communicated.						
The desired state, guided by purpose & identity, is understood by all.						
We connect all activity to the vision and the plan.						
Progress is communicated broadly and frequently.						

Executing the Plan	5	4	3	2	1	**Comments**
Resources have been assigned to projects that make up the plan						
Each Project has a charter with clear goals and objectives.						
Milestones and timing have been developed for each project.						
Each project has a "manager" who leads the team in achieving the project charter.						
The executive leadership team monitors project progress.						
Measures of progress are used for improvement, not punishment						

	Often	Somewhat		Never	
Executing the Plan - Barriers	5	4	3	2	1	**Comments**
The executive leadership team removes barriers to project progress.						
The executive leaderhip team addresses "idol" issues.						
Tradition-bound members are engaged on the purpose & identity - the why of everything that is done. Activities can be tested against the vision.						

Sustaining the Change	5	4	3	2	1	**Comments**
Principle statements reflect beliefs and expected behaviors.						
Covenants are used to empower church ministries and committees.						
Rituals reinforce the vision, purpose & identity.						
Frequest communication of success and progress occur.						
Deterrents and distractions are dealt with rapidly and with a loving approach.						
The executive committee focuses on direction, covenants, and empowerment and less on committee details.						

EXECUTING THE TRANSFORMATION MAP

There are two classes of tools for executing the projects on the transformation map – Getting Things Done and Improving the Work of the Church.

TOOLS AND PRACTICES FOR GETTING THINGS DONE

MEETINGS

Wasteful meetings are great fodder for Dilbert cartoons. Who hasn't sat through a meeting that held nothing but reports and a waste of time?

Meeting protocol in churches came about before the internet and smart phones. There was an abundance of meetings to enhance communication and to create an inclusive environment. Our meeting protocol hasn't changed with the times. Thus, it is very wasteful.

Ways to make meetings more effective (even to the point of elimination) and spiritually centered are:

Sample Agenda for a Team's First Meeting

- Christ Candle & Empty Chair
- Devotion & Opening Prayer (5-10 min.)
- Review this agenda (5 min.)
- Brief self-introductions (10 min.)
- Review the charter or mission statement (15 min.)
- Discuss the roles of the team leader, coach and team members (15 min.)
- Set ground rules (15 min.)
- Introduce basic concepts or skills needed for the work (15 min.)
- Discuss assignments for the next meeting, date, time (10 min.)
- Meeting evaluation (10 min.)
- Closing Prayer

Sample Agenda for a Team's Regular Meetings

- Christ Candle & Empty Chair
- Warm-up or check-in
- Devotion & Opening Prayer (5-10 min.)
- Agenda review
- Status reports on action items and assignments from the last meeting

- Issues to be discussed or decided, work that needs to be done with most members present
- Review progress relative to work plan and schedule.
- Assignments for work to be done in between meetings (who will do what by when)
- Reminders of upcoming special meetings or events
- Review action items from this meeting
- Draft agenda for the next meeting
- Meeting evaluation
- Closing Prayer

Key Meeting Roles
Meeting leader
- Open the meeting with Devotion
- Review the agenda
- Move through the agenda one item at a time
- Keep the team focused on the agenda
- Facilitate discussions
- Manage participation
- Help the team use appropriate decision methods
- Close the meeting.

Timekeeper
- Keep track of time during the meetings
- Alert the team when the time allocated for an item is almost up so the team can decide whether to continue the discussion, table it, or assign it to a sub-team.

Note-taker
- Capture key points for each agenda item
- Highlight decisions and action items
- Collect future agenda items
- Distribute meeting minutes and post agenda items.

Scribe
- Posts ideas on a flip chart or whiteboard.
  - Helps team stay focused on the discussion.

• Prevents "team memory" from changing during dialogue.
• Shows members that their ideas have been captured for consideration, thereby encouraging participation.

Example Ground-Rules
• Take care of yourself (restroom, emergency telephone calls, etc.)
• Honor time limits (arrive a few minutes before the meeting and respect the timekeeper.)
• Everyone's participation is needed.
• One person talks at a time.
• Each person will be able to express his or her thought without interruption
• Say what you think and feel.
• Hold yourself open to the influence of others.
• No long war stories.
• No personal attacks, no accusations—upgrade the idea that you don't like instead of attacking the person who suggested it.
• If you must leave the meeting for an emergency, make arrangements with your teammates.
• If you must miss a meeting, catch up via the meeting minutes and a team member.

Guidelines for a Team
• Keep the Great Commission and your church purpose as the primary guides.
• Help each other be right, not wrong.
• Look for ways to make new ideas work – not for reasons they won't.
• If in doubt, check out the facts; don't make assumptions.
• Speak positively about each other and about Christianity and our church at every opportunity.
• Maintain a positive mental attitude, no matter the circumstances.
• Act with prayerful confidence and courage. God is depending upon you.
• Do everything with enthusiasm – it's contagious.
• Whatever you want – give it away. (power, respect, enthusiasm, compassion, recognition, etc.)
• Don't lose faith – persevere

GUIDELINES FOR EFFECTIVE DECISIONS

Methods for Making Decisions

Consensus	Voting
When decisions are important, have large ramifications, or effect a lot of people.	When it is known that consensus is highly unlikely in the time allowed.
When groups are small (10 or fewer) you should consider consensus; with large groups you usually need consensus on issues of great importance.	When members of the group are equally informed on the subject matter and understand one another's viewpoints.
When the group is informed and individual members feel a similar level of investment or are critical to a good decision.	When it's been determined that the majority can handle the implementation without the active involvement of those who "lose" in the vote.
When consensus can't be achieved you should have a back-up method to reach a decision.	When you have a plan for how to handle those who "lose" to keep them from becoming defensive.
Subgroup	**One Person**
When a subgroup has the necessary information or expertise to make the decision.	When it is an emergency.
When a subgroup is the only entity impacted by the decision and can implement it without the active involvement of the majority.	When one person has all the relevant information.
	When one person is especially trusted to make a good decision.
When the whole group is truly comfortable delegating their authority to representatives.	When the outcome only impacts the decision maker.

What is Consensus?

Consensus does not mean:
- a unanimous vote
- everyone getting everything they want
- everyone finally coming around to the "right" opinion

Consensus does mean
- everyone understands the decision and can explain why it is best.
- everyone can live with the decision

Consensus requires
- time
- active participation of all team members
- skills in communication, listening, conflict resolution and facilitation
- creative thinking and open-mindedness

Tips for Achieving Successful Consensus
1. Listen carefully
2. Encourage all members to participate fully
3. Seek out differences of opinion
4. Search for alternatives that meet the goals of all members
5. Avoid changing your mind only to avoid a conflict
6. Don't just argue for your point of view
7. Balance power
8. Make sure there is enough time
9. Check understanding

PROJECT MANAGEMENT

In shifting the culture, you will have a number of projects that you wish to accomplish. You may choose to organize these with a Transformation Map. Like many times before, you might say: "We have great ideas, but nothing seems to ever get done." The primary reasons for this shortfall are 1) lack of basic project management skills and 2) confusing roles and accountabilities.

The culmination of the highest award in the Boy Scouts of America is the Eagle Project. It is called a project because the candidate scout has learned many skills, as illustrated by merit badges, but needs to be able to organize and execute a project through others that serves a community need. The basic project management skills that they learn are:
- Project Charter
    - What is the problem that is being solved?
    - Who benefits (stakeholder) and do they support the project?
    - What is the scope?
    - Project Objectives
    - Project Measures of Success
    - Resources – team members and $$
    - Project Deadline

- Project Plan & Schedule
    - Ensure project funding
    - Create Activities/Tasks, listed in sequence
        Larger projects may include design, procure, build, and deliver phases
    - Assign responsibility for each activity/task
    - Estimated duration of activities and tasks, taking into account that some activities/tasks can be done in parallel.
    - Identify Risks and Develop Contingency Plans for significant risks.
    - Review with Stakeholder before proceeding to Execution
- Project Execution and Monitoring
    - Hold regular team meetings to update the progress of each active step.
    - Respond to delays in task completion with recovery plans
    - On large projects, hold regular update meetings with the stakeholder.
- Project Close Out
    - Hold meeting with stakeholder to review the impact of the project (objectives and measures met?)
    - Develop lessons learned
    - Write report that summarizes the project, team members, impact and lessons learned.

This checklist works well for conducting a bazaar, installing new media capability in the sanctuary, buying new choir robes, building an addition, etc.

Clarifying Roles - RACI

RACI is a matrix that describes the participation by various roles in completing tasks or deliverables for a project or business process. RACI is an acronym derived from the four key responsibilities most typically used: responsible, accountable, consulted, and informed. It is used for clarifying and defining roles and responsibilities in cross-functional or departmental projects and processes. It reduces confusion, clarifies accountability, and speeds the process.

There is a distinction between a role and individually identified people: a role is a descriptor of an associated set of tasks; may be performed by many people; and one person can perform many roles.

R = Responsible

Those who do the work to complete the task. There is at least one role with this participation type, although others can be delegated to assist in the work required.

A = Accountable (also approver or final approving authority)

The one ultimately answerable for the correct and thorough completion of the deliverable or task, the one who ensures the prerequisites of the task are met and who delegates the work to those responsible. In other words, an accountable must sign off (approve) work that Responsible provides. There must be only one Accountable specified for each task or deliverable.

C = Consulted

Those whose opinions are sought, typically subject-matter experts; and with whom there is two-way communication.

I = Informed

Those who are kept up-to-date on progress, often only on completion of the task or deliverable; and with whom there is just one-way communication.

Very often the role that is accountable for a task or deliverable may also be responsible for completing it. This is indicated on the matrix by the task or deliverable having a role accountable for it, but no role responsible for its completion, i.e. it is implied. Outside of this exception, it is generally recommended that each role in the project or process for each task receive, at most, just one of the participation types. Where more than one participation type is shown, this generally implies that participation has not yet been fully resolved, which can impede the value of this technique in clarifying the participation of each role on each task.

RASI – modified RACI

RASI is a modification of RACI and is a matrix that describes the participation by various roles in completing tasks or deliverables for a project or business process.

R = Responsible
A = Accountable (also approver or final approving authority)
S = Support
I = Informed

An example for filling Council of Ministry Leader openings is:

ACTIVITY	BRIAN	JANE	MIKE	TOM	CAROLE	COUNCIL PRESIDENT	PASTOR	COMPLETION DATE
Assessment of current Council capabilities and gaps	R	S	I	S	I	A	I	9/1
Prospect Identification	S	S	S	S	R	A	S	9/15
Prospect Cultivation	S	R	S	S	S	A	S	10/15
Recruitment	S	R	S	S	S	A	S	11/15
Election of Ministry Leaders	S	S	S	S	S	R/A	I	12/15
Outboarding and Orientation	S	S	S	R	S	A	S	1/15

PRACTICES AND TOOLS FOR IMPROVING THE WORK OF THE CHURCH

Work Flows

Work is accomplished through processing (or transforming) an input through a number of steps to produce an output/outcome. There are many work processes in any organization.

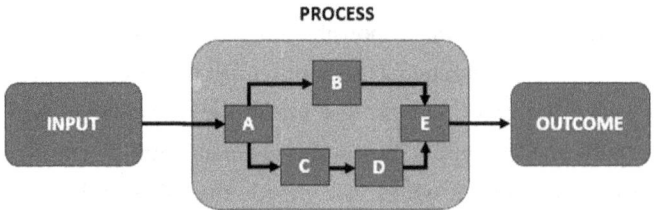

Work is made efficient and easily reproduced through a standard input and standard steps within the process. Standardization is monitored through measurement.

Work Flow (Process) Improvement

One of the ways to get more things done is to improve the work process. The improvement is seen through reduced time and effort and/or a higher quality outcome.

When a problem is simple, INTUITIVE ANALYSIS works.

1. Think about the problem and alternative solutions
2. Make a choice
3. Take action

This works well when you have sufficient background and few alternatives.

However, when the work process or the problem is complex, process improvement needs to be structured.

1. Define the customer and the problem
2. Define who is the process owner
3. Map the work flow as activity steps and who is responsible for each step.
4. Analyze each activity for improvement.
5. Make choices for improvement
6. Utilize project management skills to take action.

Measures/Metrics for Awareness and Improvement, Not Keeping Score

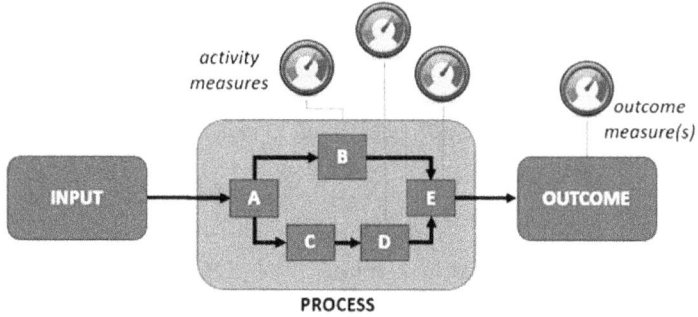

We think it is important to focus on BOTH activity measures within the process and outcome measures. Many organizations learn the cause-and-effect relationships between these two distinct measures. The activity measures become the leading indicators of outcome performance.

We also endorse a cadence of accountability – a regular review of the measures to 1) confirm performance to standard, 2) reaffirm responsibilities, and 3) reaffirm cause-and-effect relationships.

Churches have traditionally focused on activity measures, such as the number of worship attendees, giving as percent of budget, and the number of small groups. But they have done so without measuring outcomes like professions of faith, number of changed lives, etc. It is important to measure both, as activity (process) measures can be leading indicators of desired outcomes.

To some, measurement seems unspiritual. Secular applications of measurements are often punitive rather than used as a basis for improvement. Enlightened secular companies do use measures in the right way, but many companies don't. Some people maintain that you can't measure what matters in a church. But we contend that if you don't measure, you are adrift with no knowledge of where you are and where you are going. One church lost a boy Scout troop because measures and responsibilities were not in place. Poor troop leadership led to poor meetings and outings which created a downward spiral of active scouts.

Albert Einstein notably wrote: "Not everything that counts can be counted, and not everything that can be counted counts." With that in mind, here are some activity/process measures that you may consider:

WORSHIP
- Attendance as a percent of membership
- Demographics of worship attendees relative to demographics of the neighborhood

COMMUNITY SERVICE
- Ratio of ministry teams to committees
- Number of non-local church entities served
- Number of people (excluding duplicates) and percentage of attendees involved in community service
- Percent of the budget devoted to local and international missions

INDIVIDUAL DISCIPLESHIP
- Number of personal plans as a percent of membership (Personal plans should reflect the categories stated in the membership vows)
- Percent progress on personal plan (yearly summary)

CORPORATE DISCIPLESHIP
- Number of life groups and average total attendance
- Number of small groups (clear definition is required) and average total attendance
- Maturity of the small groups
- Number of Sunday School classes and average total attendance
- Number of non-Sunday morning programs for children
- Number of non-Sunday morning programs for youth

INDIVIDUAL LEADERS
- Regular prayer and Bible study
- Weekly worship attendance
- Proportional giving
- Small group participation
- Mission service (serving non-Christians)
- Personal faith sharing

CORPORATE LEADERSHIP
- Leadership position turnover
- Percent of attendees serving as leaders over the last five years

FINANCES
- Average giving per family unit
- Percentage of family units giving 75% of the church budget
- Church budget reported in a narrative format

ZONE OF DISCOMFORT / DISEQUILIBRIUM

Keeping the Fire of Change Lit Without Flameout Turning Up the Heat But Not Too Much

Individual and collective disequilibrium occur during periods of change. People like their comfort zones and "heat" is necessary to raise their disequilibrium to the point of real, sustained change (the productive zone).

Again, we acknowledge that it's like a pressure cooker: set the temperature and pressure too low, and the ingredients in the cooker will not produce a good dish. Set the temperature and pressure too high, and the lid will blow off and throw the ingredients all over the cook and the room.

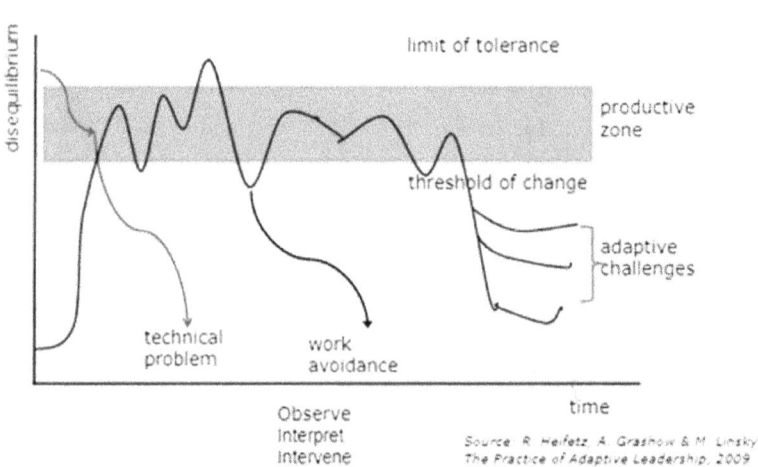

In the case of "technical problems" (building, curriculum, worship sequence, etc.) the disequilibrium lasts a short time because the solution is within the organization's structure, procedures and ways of doing things.

In the case of changes that impact people's priorities, beliefs, habits and loyalties, the change can become very onerous. People avoid the work by applying a technical solution. A prevalent example of this is electronic giving. The root cause of low generosity is the subject of this book – a truly adaptive challenge. But people get excited about making it easier to give, making the assumption that this will make it easier to give.

So changing the culture of your church is about changing priorities and behavior. They present many adaptive challenges that require adjusting the "heat" to the change.

One suggestion[36] on regulating the change is:

Increase Heat in the System	Decrease Heat in the System
• Give more responsibility – give the problem to the system.	• Address the technical aspects.
• Bring conflict into the open.	• Employ the structure
• Protect dissenting voices	• Reclaim responsibility temporarily
• Seek other perspectives	• Slow down the process.

---

[36]*Adaptive Leadership in Organizations, Future Proofing your Culture* by Joe Ellis, OnTrack International, November 2015

CHAPTER 6
LEADING – A SHARED RESPONSIBILITY

Spiritually Centered Leadership
Once the goals and processes involved in changing congregational culture become clear, the next question we ask is: "Who will lead the change?" The answer, based on our experience, is quite simple.

It has to begin with the pastor.

But—and this is a huge BUT—the pastor cannot lead alone. Much of the pastor's leadership will take the form of inspiring and enlisting other leaders and forming a cohesive leadership team, focused intently on the purpose that has been discerned.

You may recall from an earlier chapter that we spoke of the pastor shifting from serving as a spiritual shepherd to becoming a spiritual leader. Both words are important. The pastor's leadership must be anchored in a deep personal spirituality, sustained by regular spiritual disciplines and faith in God's providence.

But, by the same token, spirituality alone will not accomplish the desired cultural shift and change in the congregation. You may have known pastors (or, perhaps, been one yourself) who embodied the description of "being so heavenly minded that they were no earthly good." Conversely, leadership without spirituality can easily become a quest for advancing one's own agenda rather than seeking God's purposes.

So, we will address both elements of spiritually centered leadership and essentials for leaders in any arena. The first step for the spiritual leader is to establish a solid foundation of prayer, both personal and corporate. Any pastor or layperson seeking to lead change in the congregation will encounter barriers and resistance that could be disabling. Burnout is an ever-present danger. It will be essential to spend regular time in prayer, seeking strength and guidance from God. At the same time, this presents an opportunity to enlist the prayer warriors in the congregation, asking them to pray specifically that the pastor and lay leaders will be guided by God and provided with strength and endurance for the journey.

We believe it will also be important for the pastor to meet regularly with the leadership team for Bible study and prayer. This not only helps build community among the leaders, but also provides a constant reminder of the purpose toward which they are seeking to move the congregation. When earnestly studying and searching God's word, it becomes much more difficult to allow personal preferences to guide decision making.

It is also desirable to enlist as much of the congregation as possible in regular Bible study that focuses especially on the role of the church and God's plan for equipping everyone with gifts for ministry. The most significant shifts at Glen Mar Church while Andy was pastor were always preceded by periods of this type of church-wide Bible study. While it may be hard to "underestimate the Biblical illiteracy of the average church member," it is even more difficult to underestimate the power provided by regular corporate study of scripture.

Preaching provides another important opportunity for the spiritual leader pastor to both model and encourage the vision and purpose that have been discerned. First, of course, the pastor's own personal spiritual disciplines of prayer and study will inform her or his preaching and be evident to the congregation. Beyond that, preaching offers one of the most effective means of casting the vision of the purpose and identity and compelling members to internalize and follow the desired change.

It was Puritan preachers who first introduced the element of Application to sermons. Up to that time most preaching had relied on pure exposition of scripture. Most preaching was described as "academic" and was devoted to interpreting the meaning of scripture. The Puritans went further, however, by applying the meaning to action. Essentially, here is what it means and what it calls for the listener to do.

While teaching preaching for 15 years at Wesley Theological Seminary, Andy stressed to his students that every sermon should have both a point and a purpose. This was a lesson learned from his kindergarten teacher wife who suggested that, like any lesson, the sermon could actually have a behavioral objective. Commitment, not manipulation, was the goal, in encouraging listeners to respond to scripture by changing how they live and serve as disciples of Jesus.

A third element of the pastor's spiritual leadership is service that exemplifies a life of discipleship. At various times in his ministry, Andy engaged in what might have been regarded as menial tasks in order to remind himself that he was a servant. Sharpening pencils in pew racks, stuffing bulletins, and other chores kept him humble and in touch with God. Of course, those tasks were mostly invisible to the congregation. But we know that it is also important for the pastor to model a life of service. Andy discovered this while experiencing frustration that more members of the congregation were not taking advantage of opportunities for mission. The A-ha moment came when he realized that he, himself, had never gone on a mission trip and could not expect others to follow where he was unwilling to go.

So, through prayer, Bible study, preaching and service, the pastor provides spiritual leadership.

Types of Leaders

Not everyone is a born leader. But nearly everyone can be trained to become an effective leader. Herb Miller, in "Leadership Is the Key," puts it this way: *If medical schools can teach brain surgery, leadership is surely teachable.*[37] Like personality or spirituality, however, there is no "one size fits all" approach. Each individual will have unique characteristics and skills that can be adapted and honed for effective leadership.

We have seen many types of leaders in laity and pastors. Craig Groeschel of LifeChurch describes these different types well.[38]

1. **Unpredictable** leaders produce hesitant followers.

2. **Domineering (Directing)** leaders produce compliant followers who are NOT committed to the change.

3. **Secretive** leaders produce guarded followers who provide little feedback and therefore NO transparency about what's really happening.

4. **Passive** leaders produce disengaged followers.

5. **Healthy** leaders produce faithful followers. If you work for a healthy leader, you're going to want to follow, sacrifice, and give your best. The next type of leader, however, is a step beyond healthy.

6. **Empowering** leaders don't just produce followers—they produce other great leaders. Empowering leaders are not focused on themselves. Instead, they empower people with the ability to say, 'yes' to the Purpose & Identity, as well as its opportunities. If people deep within the organization have the ability to say, 'yes,' you have an empowering culture.

---

[37] Herb Miller, *Leadership Is the Key*, Nashville, Abingdon Press, 1997, pg. 70

[38] https://www.youtube.com/watch?v=WWlSjnYqYWA and
https://www.youtube.com/watch?v=Jpcr2GX4S-A

Situational Leadership

Something to note about types of leaders is that different situations call for different leadership styles. The response to a crisis often calls for a **Domineering** style to produce short-term results. Initially in a transformation, a **Healthy** style is needed until leadership can be developed within others. A Healthy leadership style is required where people don't have the capability to lead – a common situation in church servants. The **Empowering** style feels awkward because you are not in control and don't have the answer (sometimes unsettling to a parishioner or a District Superintendent). But with this leadership style, you can always get an answer to their questions or relay their concerns.

Ted witnessed the sad outcome of a church when a Domineering pastor succeeds an Empowering pastor. The Empowering pastor had been at the church for twenty-five years and the church had grown well. People attributed the success of the church to the pastor when, in reality, the pastor had empowered others. The incoming pastor was trained to be Domineering by the corporate church culture. Often the Domineering pastor must change things to prove his/her individual worth. This led to the empowered laity leaders leaving the church. The remaining laity blamed the pastor, and a third pastor was soon assigned. The third pastor was in a dilemma, not wanting to be directive but inheriting laity that were doers, not leaders. This churn led to a division in the congregation between those who said change was too slow and those who said change was too fast. This church struggles to this day. The root cause may go back to the successful twenty-five-year pastor who created an identity & purpose in the empowered laity leaders, but did not extend that to all in the congregation.

In conclusion, we advocate that the pastor be an EMPOWERING LEADER and that laity assume HEALTHY LEADER roles. This develops ownership of the local church within the laity, who normally far outlive the tenure of any pastor.

Biblical Models of Servant Leadership

The concept of Servant Leadership was first popularized by Robert K. Greenleaf, whose book with that title was first published in 1977. In exploring the idea of servant leadership, Greenleaf began by asking and answering a question:

Servant and leader – can these two roles be fused in one real person, in all levels of status and calling? If so, can that person live and be productive in the real world of the present? My sense of the present leads me to say yes to both questions.[39]

According to Greenleaf, the servant leader is servant first and then leader. This produces one whose first priority is that those being served grow as persons. Servant leaders are known as those who "enrich by their presence."

Biblical models for servant leadership are numerous. Moses is variously described as God's servant, My servant, and the servant of the Lord. In fact, it has been noted, the term servant is used to describe Moses more often than any other Biblical figure, including Jesus. Moses provided leadership to the Hebrew people in their flight from Egypt to the promised land but was seen (and by all accounts saw himself) as servant first and leader second.

Second Isaiah contains four so-called "Servant songs." While scholars may hold different views regarding the identity of the servant, the role of the servant is clearly to lead the people to achieve God's purpose for the world.

> *Here is my servant, whom I uphold, my chosen in whom my soul delights; I have put my spirit upon him; he will bring forth justice to the nations. He will not cry or lift up his voice, or make it heard in the street; a bruised reed he will not break, and a dimly burning wick he will not quench; he will faithfully bring forth justice. He will not grow faint or be crushed until he has established justice in the earth.*
>
> **Isaiah 42:1-4 (NRSV)**

---

[39] Robert K Greenleaf, Servant Leadership: A Journey into the Nature of Legitimate Power and Greatness, Mahwah, NJ, Paulist Press, 1977, 7

Isaiah refers to Israel as "my servant who I have chosen," who is later told that, "you are my witnesses!" The stakes become even higher in the second Servant song in Isaiah 49:

> *It is too light a thing that you should be my servant to raise up the tribes of Jacob and to restore the survivors of Israel; I will give you as a light to the nations, that my salvation may reach to the end of the earth.*
>
> **Isaiah 44:1(NRSV)**

Jesus clearly and emphatically teaches and models servant leadership, and occasionally has to set his disciples straight on their expected role. When brothers James and John came to him with the request that he "grant us to sit, one at your right hand and one at your left, in your glory," Jesus very pointedly defines servant leadership:

> *You know that among the Gentiles those whom they recognize as their rulers lord it over them, and their great ones are tyrants over them. But it is not so among you; whoever wishes to become great among you must be your servant, and whoever wishes to be first must be slave of all.*
>
> **Mark 10:42-44 (NRSV)**

And, again, in Luke Jesus identified both the disciples and himself as servants.

> *The kings of the Gentiles lord it over them; and those in authority over them are called benefactors. But not so with you; rather the greatest among you must become like the youngest, and the leader like one who serves. For who is greater, the one who is at the table or the one who serves? Is it not the one at the table? But I am among you as one who serves.*
>
> **Luke 22:25-27 (NRSV)**

Perhaps the most forceful admonition to guide servant leaders can be found in Paul's encouragement in Philippians 2 to:

> *Do nothing from selfish ambition or conceit, but in humility regard others as better than yourselves. Let each of you look not to your own interests, but to*

> *the interests of others. Let the same mind be in you that was in Christ Jesus, who though he was in the form of God, did not regard equality with God as something to be exploited, but emptied himself, taking the form of a slave.*
>
> **Philippians 2:3-7 (NRSV)**

Brooks Faulkner of Lifeway cited "Seven Biblical Models of Leadership" exemplified by individuals in scripture. These can be found online.[40]

Laity Leaders

While much of this chapter has been written addressing pastors, each of these sections apply equally to lay leaders. This is particularly important when the pastor does not have the skills to be a leader. Many parishioners will be affiliated with the church for decades, whereas the pastor may only be there for a few years. The parishioners need to be stewards of God's gift and act as kingdom builders, not kingdom dwellers.

Leadership Traits

Many of the books on leadership provide their own lists of leadership traits or characteristics. Drawing from these and other lists, as well as our own experience, we would suggest the following essential leadership qualities:

1. Integrity: say what you mean and live what you say.

2. Inspiration: the ability to communicate Purpose & Identity, goals and hopes in ways that move others toward new thinking and actions. Lovett Weems cites Peter Senge's admonition that "the essence of leadership - what we do with 98 Percent of our time - is communication."[41]

3. Authenticity and Transparency: especially important in today's culture, avoid hidden motives or secret deals

---

[40] https://www.lifeway.com/en/articles/church-leadership-seven-biblical-models September 8, 2015

[41] Lovett H. Weems, Jr., Take the Next Step: Leading Lasting Change in the Church, Nashville, Abingdon Press, 2003, 119

4. Courage: ability and willingness to make the purpose and mission the priority even when that affects relationships.

5. Energy and persistence: leading change is hard work and requires great stamina, especially in the face of resistance.

6. Consistency: Every exception, no matter how well intentioned, opens the way to a slippery slope.

7. Respect: the ability to listen to dissent but be steadfast in direction (purpose and identity.)

8. Ability to:

    a. learn from the past BUT don't live in it.

    b. live in the present BUT don't accommodate it.

    c. look to the future BUT don't wait for it.

9. Forthrightness: the courage to sensitively communicate concern for others, even when there is a risk of alienation.

10. Effective conflict and resistance management: the ability to help people reflect on the values driving their perspectives and to reconcile their desires with the purpose & identity.'

After such a comprehensive list, one might be tempted to add, "jump tall buildings in a single bound and stop speeding bullets in one's teeth." Such an imposing list could cause even the most dedicated would-be leader to give up in frustration. In reality, it is very unlikely that any one individual can possess all of these characteristics. That is why we stress the idea of partnership, creating a team that can provide leadership skills that may be lacking in the pastor in order to effectively lead fruitful change.

Leaders guide effective changes and as an Agent of Change,

    - You will live in the future and be painfully aware of the present.

    - You will always be in the process of personal development.

    - You will find yourself often being alone and feeling marginal.

    - You will find yourself experiencing higher and higher levels of resistance.

- You will get more and more in touch with what it means to "move in" and "move out".

- You will need to be caring and confrontational, guiding and directive.

- You will keep trying to see situations with different eyes.

- Edges of your patience will be pushed (nothing moves fast enough).

- You will know rejection intimately.

- You will constantly be revisiting your own values.

- You will live with the tension between blending and differentiating with the congregation.

- You will struggle between doing what the church needs and what you need.

- Your honesty with yourself will enable you to relate to others.

- You will truly be yourself only when you know yourself.

- Your greatest joy will be what you can do for others, so they can do for themselves.

- You will come to understand that we must care for ourselves because no one else really can.

As a leader, you will be seeking to move yourself and the organization into that zone of discomfort where change occurs. If you aim below the lower edge of that zone, permanent change will not occur. If you are near the upper edge of that zone, it may feel like you are on the edge of chaos. When you are nearing the edge of chaos, you will find some things that are mostly stable and some that will vary, depending on the circumstances.[42]

---

[42]Adapted from Margaret Wheatley, "Leading in Times of Chaos", 1994 Conference of Organizational Systems Designers

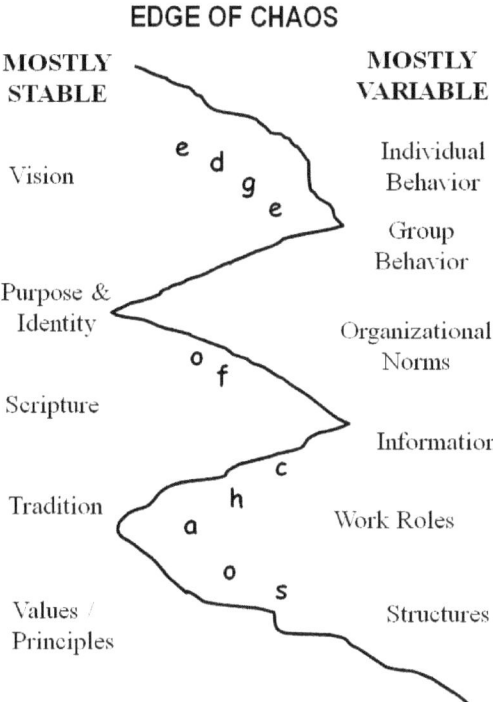

The Cost of Leadership

In his book *Failure of Nerve*[43], Edwin Friedman comments that he had opportunity to observe families and institutions repeat the same problems while serving as a pulpit rabbi and family therapist in the Washington, DC, area for nearly 40 years. These experiences led him to develop very specific understandings of the qualities that create effective leaders.

After describing leadership as primarily an emotional process Friedman states that "A leader must separate his or her own emotional being from that of his or her followers while still remaining connected. Vision is basically an emotional rather than a cerebral phenomenon, depending more on a leader's capacity to deal with anxiety than his or her professional training or degree. A leader needs

---

[43] Friedman, Edwin H., A Failure of Nerve: Leadership in the Age of the Quick Fix – 10th Edition, New York, Church Publishing, 1999, 2007, 2017.

the capacity not only to accept the solitariness that comes with the territory. He says that leaders must be willing to be vulnerable, to not fear criticism or the sense of being alone in taking responsibility. "Leaders must not only not be afraid of that position; they must come to love it."

Friedman stresses the value of a well-differentiated leader, "I mean someone who can be separate while still remaining connected, and therefore can maintain a modifying, non-anxious, and sometimes challenging presence. I mean someone who can manage his or her own reactivity to the automatic reactivity of others, and therefore be able to take stands at the risk of displeasing."

Perhaps most importantly for church leaders he claims that, "In any type of institution whatsoever, when a self-directed, imaginative, energetic, or creative member is being consistently frustrated and sabotaged rather than encouraged and supported, what will turn out to be true one hundred percent of the time, regardless of whether the disrupters are supervisors, subordinates, or peers, is that the person at the very top of that institution is a peace-monger. By that I mean a highly anxious risk-avoider, someone who is more concerned with good feelings than with progress, someone whose life revolves around the axis of consensus… someone who functions as if she had been filleted of her backbone."

In the chapter on Culture we stress the importance of knowing one's own personal culture, as well as the language, images, norms and rituals that guide decisions and actions. This is one important aspect of knowing one's self and becoming the kind of self-differentiated leader Friedman lauds. Also important is an accurate assessment of one's strengths and weaknesses and a willingness to compensate for weak areas by enlisting others.

Only this kind of self-knowledge enables one to lead with integrity, transparency and consistency.

Leadership is not for the faint of heart. Everyone who seeks to lead, especially leading culture change in a congregation, should be prepared for resistance, sabotage, apathy and many sleepless nights. Some specific forms of resistance and barriers will be addressed in the next chapter. And we will suggest strategies for the care and feeding of clergy and lay leaders in a subsequent chapter.

Turning again to Friedman's work, we find five aspects of leadership that he attributes to early explorers and claims are essential for leaders of any social system.

1. A capacity to get outside the emotional climate of the day. Vision, he says, is the ability to see things differently, having some sense of where you begin and end.

2. A willingness to be exposed and vulnerable. More than a fear of criticism, leaders must be able to face the anxiety of being alone and having to take total responsibility. Leaders, he says, "must not only not be afraid of that position; they must come to love it."

3. Persistence in the face of resistance and downright rejection. Leadership, according to Friedman, requires a kind of relentless drive toward purpose when meeting resistance from others and even from within oneself.

4. Stamina in the face of sabotage along the way. In all likelihood even some who are initially enthusiastic about the mission will fall away as hardships are encountered.

5. Headstrong and ruthless. This involves being committed to the mission and not allowing relationships to get in the way.[44]

Leading Others

The first rule in leading others is to know yourself and be authentic. As previously mentioned, Ted learned this in his business career when a 360-degree evaluation was conducted of his performance. He received his lowest marks from those who reported to him. When he met with his group to understand why, they initially hesitated in being honest with their comments. Once Ted made it safe for them to be honest, they told him that he appeared to be putting on a show rather than demonstrating authenticity. They also suggested that he was getting stuck on key details rather than seeing the end-goal. The one-hour feedback session was

---

[44] Friedman, Failure of Nerve, 188-89

the most difficult hour of Ted's business career. But it made a difference in his approach to work and to life.

Ted's engineering background blinded him from seeing his mindset and behavior. The behavior you see is guided by mental models, values and principles, and needs and fears.

Be aware of your mental models and recognize how they help you see the world but also how they filter the information you receive. As you are self-aware of your mental models, you can begin to see other's mental models and, more importantly, how those models guide the person's perspectives. A useful tool is the Myers-Briggs Type Indicators (MBTI). We will introduce how different MBTI types respond to change and you will see the enormity of different responses to change in Chapter 7.

Values and the corresponding principles that guide behavior can be stated, but they are truly defined during a crisis or unsettling change. When you meet with someone during the transformation regarding their resistance or reluctance, you have the opportunity to explore their values, needs and fears with them. Your willingness to listen to them and understand where they are coming from will enable you to be a leader in their eyes.

Others will change their mindsets and behavior if leaders role model, foster understanding and conviction, develop talent and skills, and reinforce with formal mechanisms as discussed by McKinsey & Company. [45]

---

[45] Basford, Tessa and Schaninger, Bill, McKinsey Quarterly, "The Four Building Blocks of Change", April 2016

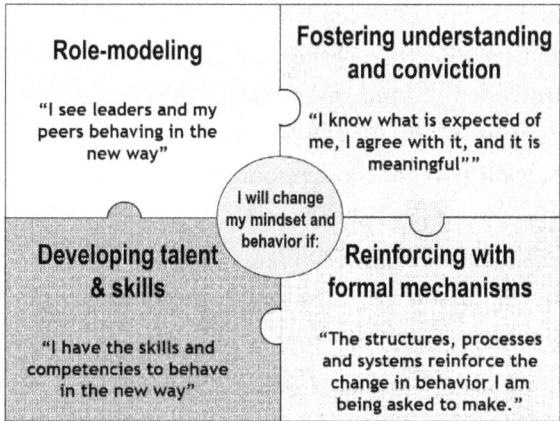

ROLE MODELING – I see leaders and my peers behaving in a new way.
- Setting the example in interactions with one another.
- Holding each other accountable for "walking the talk".
- Tactfully and actively challenging the status quo.
- Role modeling faith and courage.
- Actively managing resistance and conflict.

FOSTERING UNDERSTANDING AND CONVICTION – I know what is expected of me, I agree with it, and it is meaningful.
- Using themes to develop a compelling change story.
- Engaging in dialogue to make the story real; helping personalize the story and what it means to others.
- Seeking input from the congregation.
- Uncovering and addressing hidden concerns and competing efforts.
- Celebrating success stories.

DEVELOPING TALENT & SKILLS – I have the skills and competencies to behave in the new way.
- Diagnosing capability needs and gaps.
- Developing capabilities through coaching and feedback.
- Holding each other accountable for developing self and others.
- Matching the right people to critical jobs.
- Building a network of change agents.
- Importing external perspectives.

REINFORCING WITH FORMAL MECHANISMS – The structures, processes and systems reinforce the change in behavior I am being asked to make.
- Clarifying structure, roles and governance as the change evolves.
- Establishing targets and metrics for success.
- Making sure people have the tools, resources and authority they require.
- Recognizing people for desired behaviors.
- Ensuring follow-up and accountability.

LIVE IT OUT

- Watch the following episodes from the Lewis Center for Church Leadership

    Episode 18

    "Hyrum Smith Shares Principles for Leading with Purpose"

    Episode 23

    "Biblical Leadership" featuring Denise Dombkowski Hopkins

    Episode 24

    "Leadership Lessons from Lovett Weems"

    Episode 37

    "Learning about Leadership from Women in the Bible" featuring Carla Works

- Assess your own leadership style. If a pastor, what would you need to change to be an Empowering Leader? If laity, what would it take for you to become a Healthy Leader?

- What could you do to become more of a Servant Leader?

CHAPTER 6
LEADING – A SHARED RESPONSIBILITY
TOOLS

The Tools include:
- Bible Verses on Leadership
- Thoughts about "A Failure of Nerve: Leadership in the Age of the Quick Fix"
- Johari Window – a Framework about Relationships

The prayer and scripture are offered for spiritual grounding as you use these tools.

PRAYER

God, you know me better than I know myself. You know my strength and faults, my desires and frustrations. Help me to better understand myself so that I can more effectively lead others in living as your disciples. At the same time, help me to see others as you see them, to view them as precious children of God with gifts for service and ministry. Guide me that I might lead in the name of Jesus. Amen.

BIBLE VERSES ON LEADERSHIP[46]

Ministry Advice offers resources and tools for Christian leaders. Their article "50 Bible Verses on Leadership" contains verses and commentary on trust in God, integrity, humility, service, confidence in the future, stamina, self-discipline, wisdom, and many more. We have included several as examples. We encourage you to read all fifty at their web site.

1. A leader's integrity comes from within
    And David shepherded them with integrity of heart; with skillful hands he led them.
    Psalm 78:72

Our words are a strong indicator of our heart's condition. It's important that we pay attention to it because strong leadership will come from the integrity of our hearts.

2. Leaders are made in troubled times
    If you falter in a time of trouble, how small is your strength!
    Proverbs 24:10

---

[46]https://www.scribd.com/document/414430138/50-Bible-Verses-on-Leadership-docx

Hopefully, you didn't aspire to leadership to walk an easy path. Leaders are needed when the road gets rockiest, and the way is unsure. A leader's mettle is truly tested in the most challenging moments.

3. Leaders practice humility
> *Not so with you. Instead, whoever wants to become great among you must be your servant*
>
> **Matthew 20:26**

4. Leaders aren't restricted by their limitations
> *Jesus replied, "What is impossible with man is possible with God."*
>
> **Luke 18:27**

Don't fall into the trap of avoiding things that are beyond your ability. The sooner you get to a place where you're no longer relying on your strengths, the sooner you're going to see God doing amazing things. If you're in your comfort zone, your leadership is compromised.

5. A real leader is the servant of all
> *"You call me 'Teacher' and 'Lord,' and rightly so, for that is what I am. Now that I, your Lord and Teacher, have washed your feet, you also should wash one another's feet. I have set you an example that you should do as I have done for you. Very truly I tell you, no servant is greater than his master, nor is a messenger greater than the one who sent him. Now that you know these things, you will be blessed if you do them."*
>
> **John 13:13–17**

Jesus isn't asking his followers to humble themselves in grand and figurative ways. He literally wants us to get on our hands and knees and serve those who follow us. No job, task, or act of service is beneath you. And while good leaders delegate, make sure you aren't delegating yourself out of all the most humbling experiences.

6. Leadership is about stamina
   Let us not become weary in doing good, for at the proper time we will reap a harvest if we do not give up.

   Galatians 6:9

A leader works hard making long-term energy investments on which they won't see an immediate return. It can be draining to be planting seeds with the hope that they'll grow into something majestic. A church or organization doesn't become efficient or productive overnight, so a leader needs to be committed to the journey.

7. Leadership isn't faint-hearted
   For the Spirit God gave us does not make us timid, but gives us power, love and self-discipline.

   2 Timothy 1:7

If we look to Jesus as a model of leadership, we're instantly struck by his courage. He has so many opportunities to backpedal or recant. He presses on towards his goal.

The same Spirit that strengthened Jesus, strengthens us. When we learn to lean into that strength, our leadership abides in his power, love, and self-discipline.

8. A leader turns to God for wisdom
   If any of you lacks wisdom, you should ask God, who gives generously to all without finding fault, and it will be given to you.

   James 1:5

INSIGHTS FROM A FAILURE OF NERVE[47]

Leadership in the Age of the Quick Fix

In the chapter titled "The Problem with Leadership," Edwin Friedmen indicates that while coaching members of various professions and listening to them a

---

[47] Edwin Friedman, Failure of Nerve: Leadership in the Age of the Quick Fix, New York, Seabury Books, 2007, 13-14.

universal law of leadership began to formulate itself. He describes it in this way: "In any type of institution whatsoever, when a self-directed, imaginative, energetic, or creative member is being consistently frustrated and sabotaged rather than encouraged and supported, what will turn out to be true one hundred percent of the time, regardless of whether the disrupters are supervisors, subordinates, or peers, is that the person at the very top of that institution is a peace monger. By that I mean a highly anxious risk avoider, someone who is more concerned with good feelings than with progress, someone whose life revolves around the axis of consensus, a 'middler,' someone who is incapable of taking well-defined stands that his disability seems to be genetic, someone who functions as if she had been filleted of backbone, someone who treats conflict or anxiety like mustard gas--one whiff, on goes the emotional gas mask and he flits. Such leaders are nice if not charming." Later Friedman says, "I want to stress that by well-differentiated leader I do not mean an autocrat who tells others what to do or orders them around...Rather, I mean someone who has clarity about his or her own life goals, and, therefore, someone who is less likely to become lost in the anxious emotional processes swirling about. I mean someone who can be separate while still remain connected, and therefore can maintain a modifying, non-anxious, and sometimes challenging presence. I mean someone who can mange his or her own reactivity to the automatic reactivity of others, and therefore be able to take stands at the risk of displeasing."

THE JOHARI WINDOW

A Framework about Relationships

Adapted from written and personal study by Felicia Trecek. 07/06/2013 (revised 07/09/2013) and enhanced by Ted Brown

Messiah [Christ] said we are to love our enemies (Matt 5:43-48). Yet we see people all around us incapable of getting along with their friends or family members. Hate, anger, jealousy, resentment, and the like reside in too many self-proclaimed Christians. What is the problem? There is one very general answer which is: sin. However, 'sin' is too broad of an answer.

All Bible readers know that hate, unjustifiable and/or prolonged anger, jealousy, resentment, and the like are not fruits of the Righteous Spirit. Intellectually and based upon a plethora of information that is available to us today, we all know negative emotions are unhealthy for us. This being true, why do many self-proclaiming Christians hold onto hate, anger, jealousy, resentment, and the like? The answer: past hurts, insecurities and/or pride. Anger can be, for example, a cover-up, or rather a self-defense mechanism for pain. Anger can also stem from pride. For another example: jealousy can stem from insecurity.

Before delving too far into emotional self-discovery and overcoming, we must ask ourselves important questions. Why is examining oneself so vitally important for a Christian? Can't we just give our heart to Jesus, and everything is just wonderful and dandy now? Jesus loves me! Jesus will save me from everything by doing all the work for me...right? Can I just go to church once a week, warm a seat, sing a few songs, feel warm and fuzzy, and believe I am going to heaven? What's wrong with this picture?

Each Individual Christian Needs to be Honest with Themselves
The apostle Paul admonishes us to examine ourselves. 2 Cor. 13:5 reads, "Examine yourselves to see whether you are in the faith; test yourselves". Some people might think they are in the faith, but are truly not. There are others who play games with themselves — people who know they do things that are contrary to the faith, but do very little or nothing to change it.

The Johari Window is a helpful tool for understanding ourselves.

Johari Window
Back in 1955 two men came up with a model to help people discuss various aspects of self-awareness. It's called The Johari Window (the word 'JoHari' is a combination of the two people's first names, Joseph & Harry). The four quadrants of the Johari Window clarify whether information about self is known or unknown to either self or others. The below chart shows each of these quadrants.[48]

---

[48] https://en.wikipedia.org/wiki/Myers%E2%80%93Briggs_Type_Indicator

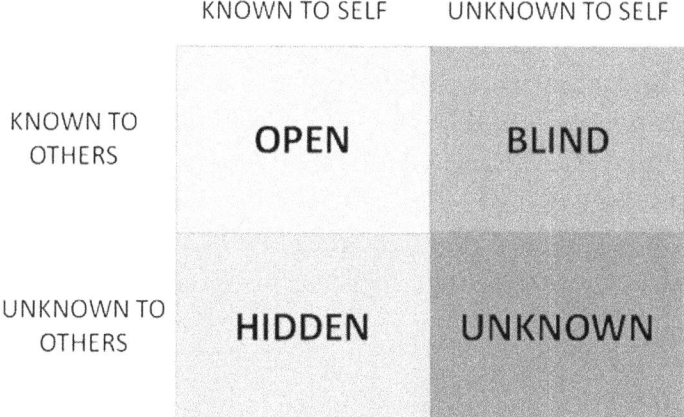

Open Self: Known to self and others.
This quadrant represents what people know about you and what you know about you. It is common knowledge that is usually easily accessible. It might include information that people can learn from you (ex. your beliefs or views), information that others can observe (ex. your appearance, behaviors, or skills) or information that is available to the public (ex. your birthday, family info, email address, etc.).

Blind Self: Unknown to self but known to others.
This quadrant reveals what people know about you and what you do not know about yourself. Another term often associated with this quadrant is 'Blind Spots'. This is where our ignorance can truly hurt us. Others may see our weaknesses, flaws, even strengths or gifts, but they either assume you already know about it or choose not to tell you. You are left in the dark and don't even know it, a great definition of "ignorant."

Hidden Self: Known to self, but unknown to others.
The "Hidden Self" quadrant represents what we know about ourselves but conceal or hide from others. This could include practical information, like passwords or retirement funds. But most often it involves hidden feelings, sensitivities, fears, hidden agendas, etc. On occasion, we might know something about ourselves and think everyone else knows, when they really don't.

Unknown Self: Unknown to either self or others.
This final quadrant includes what is unknown to everyone, other than God Himself. These things may include feelings, attitudes, capabilities, beliefs, fears or aptitudes. Some of these things may be near the surface and readily accessible to you if you were to delve into them. Others may remain hidden for the rest of your life. Some of the best ways to unveil information in this category is to expose yourself to counseling or coaching and remain steadfast as a learner, reading books, taking classes and continuing to expand who you are and what you know.

When the OPEN quadrant is small (meaning a person discloses very little information about themselves), they are less receptive to feedback and ideas. When the OPEN quadrant is large, the more receptive they are to feedback and ideas.

Leaders try to enlarge the OPEN box by informing others and asking for feedback.

A BIBLICAL EXAMPLE OF A MAN POSSESSING A SIN IN HIS BLIND QUADRANT

In Mark 10:17-22, a rich man came to Christ and asked Him, "what shall I do that I may inherit eternal life?" Christ answered by quoting five of the ten commandments that are associated with human relationships. He quoted commandments 5-9, save number 10. Then, the rich man answered and said, "Master, all these I have observed from my youth." Then, Christ told the rich man, you lack one: go and sell everything you have, give to the poor, and come follow Me." At that moment, the rich man became very sad and walked away. Christ pointed out a sin in the rich man's blind quadrant.

The rich man was violating the last commandment: "thou shalt not covet." Although in reality, the rich man was violating the first commandment also.

Coveting is a form of idolatry. Christ said in Matthew 6:24, "No one can serve two masters. Either you will hate the one and love the other, or you will be devoted to the one and despise the other. You cannot serve both God and money." In the case of the rich man, he was unable to follow Christ because he placed more value upon his possessions.

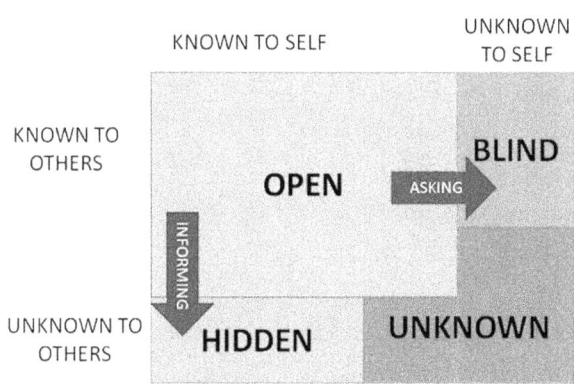

How to Reveal the Hidden and Blind Areas

Christ/Messiah said in Matthew 7:3, "Why do you look at the speck of sawdust in your brother's eye and pay no attention to the plank in your own eye?" The plank Christ/Messiah is speaking about most likely resides in the Johari Window "blind" or "unknown" quadrant. Every human being has had or continues to have a big plank in their own eye in some aspect or area in their life. As Christians, it's our personal responsibility to take out the planks in our own eye as Christ/Messiah instructed us in Matthew 7:5. "You hypocrite, first take the plank out of your own eye, and then you will see clearly to remove the speck from your brother's eye." In other words, don't have the mindset that YHWH will somehow miraculously take out your planks for you. It's our responsibility to take out our own planks. And in order to see our planks, we need to make our "OPEN" quadrant larger and accept feedback from other people.

The means to reveal "what is unknown to others" as well as understand "what others see but you are blind to" comes through small groups. A small group

consists of six to twelve people (singles, men, women, couples, etc.) who are shepherded by a facilitator for:
Spiritual disciplines
Maintaining confidentiality
Asking others to help me stay true to my Christian resolutions, accountability
Love / Caring
Like interests, similar stages of life

Growth in faith, growth as a disciple
Reading and study of Scripture
Outreach to each other in support
Uplifting joys, sorrows, and fears
Praying for each other and for the church

Relationships are the Weightier Matters of the Law

Christ/Messiah said in Matthew 5:20... " For I tell you that unless your righteousness surpasses that of the Pharisees and the teachers of the law, you will certainly not enter the kingdom of heaven." In Matthew 23:23, we learn what Christ/Messiah meant in Matthew 5:20 - our righteousness needs to exceed that of the scribes and Pharisees. In Matthew 23:23, Christ/Messiah told the Pharisees that they were hypocrites. They pay tithe of mint, dill and cumin, but they omit the weightier matters of the law which are: 1)judgement, 2)mercy, and 3)faith. The first two in the list (judgement and mercy) pertain to human relationships. The last, "faith" pertains the relationship with YHWH. In other words: THE WEIGHTIER MATTERS OF THE LAW ABSOLUTELY PERTAIN TO RELATIONSHIPS! Paraphrased in yet another way: if we, as Christians, do not integrate and infuse the right kind of judgement, mercy and faith, we will NOT enter the Kingdom of Heaven.

Improving Our Relationships

Returning to Matthew 7:3-5...It's our responsibility to take out our own planks in our eye. And, the way to see our planks is to make our "OPEN" quadrant larger. There are several methods to making our "OPEN" quadrant larger. We can read and educate ourselves about human relationships. Another method is to accept feedback from other people. We can ask other people for input. Or people may volunteer input without being asked. Either way, a non-defensive and non-confrontational response to feedback would be: "Thank you for caring about me. I will consider and think about what you have said." This statement does not mean that you agree or disagree with what you have just been told. However, it does allow us to honestly see how others view us. Additionally, it validates the person who is giving feedback.

The following is an exercise you might want to try:
- Make a personal rule list for yourself.
- Think about conflict situations in your past. What did you do or say? How could you have handled the situation for a better outcome? The purpose for this exercise is to facilitate a better and more positive outcome for future confrontations. Consider various conflict resolutions.

The apostle James instructed us to confess our sins to one-another in James 5:16. (See also 1-John1:9) The Spiritual tool that will give us the strength to do this is "HUMILITY." This facilitates feedback so that we can hopefully overcome our weakness. And it also facilitates the release of negative energy that compiles within us. That negative energy is called, "guilt."

CHAPTER 7
DEALING WITH PEOPLE

The Challenge of People in the Change Process

The community that your church serves has probably been changing over time. In fact, your local church may have been changing over time. The change is often slow and imperceptible. Then one day, you look and you discover that the church doesn't have the vitality it once had. Whatever happened to the Wednesday night dinners and class meetings? Where did all the Sunday School teachers go? What happened to the Boy Scout troop we used to have? Where have all the children gone? The list goes on and on for some churches.

You discover that the culture of the congregation has changed. You find that people don't commit like they used to. Why can't things be like they used to be? I didn't sign up for my leadership role to do the hard stuff.

Hopefully, you can see some ways to change the culture of your faith community. So, a dedicated team of leaders begins moving forward and suddenly ask themselves, "Why don't people see it the same way I do?"

In this chapter, we will talk about knowing others with some tools that will answer the question, "Why don't people see it the same way I do?"

Let's start with a few quotes about change.
- The world as we have created it is a process of our thinking. It cannot be changed without changing our thinking. -Albert Einstein
- Any change, even a change for the better, is always accompanied by drawbacks and discomforts. -Arnold Bennett
- When you're finished changing, you're finished. -Benjamin Franklin
- The price of doing the same old thing is far higher than the price of change. -Bill Clinton
- If you don't like change, you will like irrelevance even less. -General Eric Shinseki
- Change means that what was before wasn't perfect. People want things to be better. -Esther Dyson
- Those who cannot change their minds cannot change anything. -George Bernard Shaw
- I cannot say whether things will get better if we change; what I can say is they must change if they are to get better. -Georg C. Lichtenberg
- People can cry much easier than they can change. -James Baldwin
- Change is the law of life. And those who look only to the past or present are certain to miss the future. -John F. Kennedy
- Faced with the choice between changing one's mind and proving that there is no need to do so, almost everyone gets busy on the proof. -John Kenneth Galbraith
- Be the change that you wish to see in the world. -Mahatma Gandhi
- If you don't like something, change it. If you can't change it, change your attitude. -Maya Angelou

- I alone cannot change the world, but I can cast a stone across the waters to create many ripples. -Mother Teresa
- Change your thoughts and you change your world. -Norman Vincent Peale
- People don't resist change. They resist being changed. -Peter Senge
- You never change things by fighting the existing reality. To change something, build a new model that makes the existing model obsolete. -R. Buckminster Fuller
- Our dilemma is that we hate change and love it at the same time; what we really want is for things to remain the same but get better. -Sydney J. Harris

We will give you tools that first help answer the question: "How do I personally react to change?" You must answer that question for yourself; otherwise, you will end up playing a role and not demonstrating authenticity. People don't follow inauthentic leaders, as seen through Ted's evaluation experience previously mentioned.

So how does one get to know oneself? Out of four frameworks, Ted uses the Myers-Briggs Type Indicator (MBTI) because it works for him. He has used it to better understand himself, his colleagues at work, and family members. Andy also uses MBTI.

The Myers–Briggs Type Indicator (MBTI)[49] is based on an introspective self-report questionnaire indicating differing psychological (psychology is the science of mind and behavior) preferences in how people perceive the world and make decisions. There is controversy that Katharine Cook Briggs and her daughter Isabel Briggs Myers, creators of MBTI, were writers and not psychologists. Even though they were not trained psychologists, their MBTI tool works for Ted.

---

[49] The Myers and Briggs Foundation. (n.d.). MBTI Basics. The Myers & Briggs Foundation – MBTI© basics. Retrieved January 20,2023, from https://www.myersbriggs.org/my-mbti-personality-type/mbti-basics/

The self-administered test attempts to assign four categories: introversion or extraversion, sensing or intuition, thinking or feeling, judging or perceiving. One letter from each category is taken to produce a four-letter test result, such as "INFJ" or "ENFP"[50]. Therefore, there are sixteen (16) categories. The Keirsey Temperament Sorter uses the same categories.

MBTI allows a person to build awareness about their preferences, strengths and weaknesses in areas such as:

- Contributions to organizations
- Best ways to acknowledge contribution
- Leadership style
- Potential pitfalls and areas of growth/development
- How others may see them
- Learning style

Ted's ENTJ preferences have changed little over time:

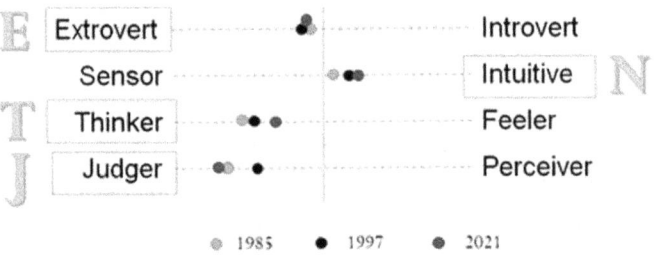

He is aware that he may overlook people's needs in his focus on task; may form decisions too quickly and appear impatient; and may ignore and suppress his own feelings. He self-reflects on his leadership style with these potential pitfalls in mind.

---

[50]Be aware that N=intuition

Andy, an INTJ, shares many of the same challenges along with the need to provide sufficient time for his introvert self to recharge and revitalize.

Some famous people in history may help you understand the MBTI framework (drawn from multiple sources):

MBTI has also been used to help preachers understand how their sermons might be perceived by different types in the congregation. It has also been used to improve awareness of perspectives in areas of conflict.

It is also useful in problem solving to have different personalities involved as they bring different perspectives.

Sensors:
 - What are the facts?
 - What exactly is the situation?
 - How would an outsider look at this situation?

Thinkers
 - What are the pros and cons of each possible solution?
 - What are the consequences of each possibility, including no action?
 - What is the cost of each possibility?

Intuitives
- What are the possibilities?
- What other ways are there for solving this problem?
- What is the problem analogous to?

Feelers
- How much will I gain or lose with each possibility?
- How will the people react to each outcome?
- How will each outcome contribute to the individual and to the group?

It is not unusual for pastors to encounter difficulty in leading a congregation because of personality differences. Numerous studies have shown that 50% of clergy in mainline Protestant churches fall into the NF category. In contrast, only 10-12% of the general population are so classified.

NF pastors are the ones most likely to fall under the need to be liked and to please everyone. "F preachers will more likely choose to be tactful rather than have people face the stark truth—and this tendency becomes greater the longer they stay in a congregation."[51]

While NF and NT pastors tend to excel in holding out a vision and inspiring others to join them, they are not usually gifted at designing or implementing processes to carry out the vision. SJ pastors are best equipped for leading these logistical and strategic efforts because of their attention to detail.

What Andy (who is an NT) found essential was to make sure the SJ personality was represented in other pastoral or lay leaders. As the church grew, one of his greatest assets became the church administrator who was able to get things done to move the church forward in pursuing the discerned vision.

---

[51] Roy Oswald & Otto Kroeger, Personality Type and Religious Leadership, The Alban Institute, 1988, 47.

In cases where there are multiple staff members, we have found it useful, if not essential, to have all staff discover their personality type. We then discuss how their differences affect the way they function as a team. While it may be a stretch to expect lay leaders to participate in such an effort, the wise pastor will try to have at least some awareness of the personality types of lay leaders and seek a diversity of types among the leadership team. Their diversity of perspectives enables creative solutions, enhances planning and problem solving, and brings a balanced approach to transformation.

While pastors of any personality type can learn to lead change by effectively surrounding themselves by those with other personality types , it could be argued that it is the NT pastor who is best equipped to lead culture change in the congregation.

As Oswald and Kroeger explain, "For NT clergy a congregation's identity is its raison d'etre—its reason for being…Most NT clergy want their congregation's identity tied to the future. The congregation is its vision of the future. NT clergy will continually hammer away at their congregation to change how they envision their future. Their primary task will be raising people's expectations so they can eventually emerge into this new future."[52]

For this reason, Andy got used to the complaint from many in the congregation that, "the only thing constant around here is change." Obviously, the NT pastor must be sensitive to trying to move people too far too fast. Andy added a pronounced NF pastor to the staff in order to help people deal with feelings of loss and threat in the midst of rapid and often dramatic change.

---

[52] Oswald and Kroeger, 173

How People React to Change

But we want to illustrate what different personality types need during times of change.

Extraverts
- Time to talk about what is going on
- Involvement – something to do
- To be heard and paid attention to; to have a voice

Introverts
- Time to reflect on what is going on
- To be asked what they think about things, often one-to-one
- Thought-out, written communications

Sensors
- Why is change occurring
- Specifics and details about the change
- Connections between the changes and the past

Intuitives
- The rationale
- A general plan to mentally play around with
- The opportunity to participate in designing the future

Thinkers
- What systemic change will there be?
- Clarity in decision making and planning of the change
- What are the goals?

Feelers
- Recognition of the impact of change on people
- What values underlie the changes?
- Demonstration that leadership cares

Judgers
- Time frames and outcomes for each stage of a concise plan of action
- A clear statement of priorities
- No surprises

Perceivers
- An open-ended plan
- Flexibility with options to choose from
- Trust in the process and calm during stormy periods

[53]

As you can see from this list of needs, people have different needs during change! Therefore, it is so important for leaders to be authentic and to consistently connect people to the Purpose & Identity that you have discerned for your church in ways that make sense to their personality type.

There are many frameworks for categorizing personalities. They are really mental models. As we said before, all mental models are wrong, but some are useful. You should choose the personality tool that best fits your team and your situation.

---

[53] Summary notes of "The Challenge of Change in Organizations: Helping Employees Thrive in the New Frontier" by Nancy J Barger and Linda K Kirby, 1995

MODES OF BEHAVIOR

Two other frameworks/mental models that Ted has found useful during a change process are reactive/ego/purposeful modes of behavior.

- Reactive speaks for itself – you react on your base instincts and sometimes do things or say things that you later regret. Ego is a more thoughtful mode where one behaves in their own self-interest. Purposeful behavior means that one is serving a higher purpose than self. Ego and higher purposes could still be idols, replacing God as our guide and counselor.

- The accompanying tool of self-observing and self-remembering is useful in seeing yourself in the moment. Ted tries to use it to temper his human nature and act in a way that is expected by his Lord and those he influences. It triggers the move from reactive to ego to purposeful behavior. It is the means of slowing down the thinking process.

CHAPTER 7
DEALING WITH PEOPLE
TOOLS

The Myers–Briggs Type Indicator (MBTI) has been discussed and the following information elaborates on this tool.

The prayer and scripture are offered for spiritual grounding as you use these tools.

PRAYER

> PRAYER: Father God, you have called us to be brothers and sisters, but sometimes we fight like dogs and cats. Instead of mutual understanding and respect we reflect suspicion, bitterness and a spirit of competition. Lead us to an attitude of mutual respect that seeks to understand both ourselves and others better and to see and treat one another as Jesus would. In his holy name we pray, Amen.

SCRIPTURE

"A new command I give you: Love one another. As I have loved you, so you must love one another. By this everyone will know that you are my disciples, if you love one another."

John 13:34-35

All the believers were one in heart and mind. No one claimed that any of their possessions was their own, but they shared everything they had. With great power the apostles continued to testify to the resurrection of the Lord Jesus. And God's grace was so powerfully at work in them all that there were no needy persons among them. For from time to time those who owned land or houses sold them, brought the money from the sales and put it at the apostles' feet, and it was distributed to anyone who had need.

Rom 15:1-7

We who are strong ought to bear with the failings of the weak and not to please ourselves. Each of us should please our neighbors for their good, to build them up. For even Christ did not please himself but, as it is written: "The insults of those who insult you have fallen on me." For everything that was written in the past was written to teach us, so that through the endurance taught in the Scriptures and the encouragement they provide we might have hope.

May the God who gives endurance and encouragement give you the same attitude of mind toward each other that Christ Jesus had, so that with one mind and one voice you may glorify the God and Father of our Lord Jesus Christ.

Accept one another, then, just as Christ accepted you, in order to bring praise to God.

Myers Briggs Type Indicator

Ref. "Please Understand Me – Character & Temperament Types", David Keirsey and Marilyn Bates, Gnosology Books ltd. 1984

Ref. "Introduction to Type 5th Ed.", Isabel Briggs Myers, Consulting Psychologists Press, 1993

Ref. "A Quick Guide to Working Together with the Sixteen Types", Linda V. Berens and Olaf Isachsen, Telos Publications, 1992

There are many mental models to help deal with a variety of people – DISC Personality Test, Strengths Finder™, Enneagram, CliftonStrengths, etc.

The mental model that we describe here is Myers Briggs Type Indicator (MBTI). Ted Brown has found it useful in business, church, and his own family. There is much written about MBTI so we will highlight some of its usefulness.

Myers–Briggs Type Indicator (MBTI) is an introspective self-report questionnaire indicating differing psychological preferences in how people perceive the world and make decisions.] The test attempts to assign four categories: introversion or extraversion, sensing or intuition, thinking or feeling, judging or perceiving. One letter from each category is taken to produce a four-letter test result, such as "INTJ" or "ESFP".

Therefore, there are sixteen different MBTI categories:

Introvert Sensing Thinking Judging	Introvert Sensing Feeling Judging	Introvert N-Intuition Feeling Judging	Introvert N-Intuition Thinking Judging
Introvert Sensing Thinking Perceiving	Introvert Sensing Feeling Perceiving	Introvert N-Intuition Feeling Perceiving	Introvert N-Intuition Thinking Perceiving
Extrovert Sensing Thinking Perceiving	Extrovert Sensing Feeling Perceiving	Extrovert N-Intuition Feeling Perceiving	Extrovert N-Intuition Thinking Perceiving
Extrovert Sensing Thinking Judging	Extrovert Sensing Feeling Judging	Extrovert N-Intuition Feeling Judging	Extrovert N-Intuition Thinking Judging

The distribution of people across each category is:

6%	6%	1%	1%
6%	6%	1%	1%
13%	13%	5%	5%
13%	13%	5%	5%

A brief description of each category is:

Overseer Inspector	Provider Protector	Forseer Developer	Director Strategist
Maneuver Operator	Performer Compositor	Proponent Advocate	Inventor Designer
Maneuver Promotor	Performer Entertainer	Proponent Messenger	Inventor Improvisor
Overseer Supervisor	Provider Guardian	Forseer Mobilizer	Director Commandant

A diverse team of people bring several different approaches to problem solving:

Sensing

- What are the facts?
- What exactly is the situation?
- What has been done?
- What am I and others doing?
- How would an outsider look at this situation?

Intuitive(N)

- What are the possibilities?
- What other ways are there for solving this problem?
- What does the data imply?
- What is this problem analogous to?

Thinking (T)

- What are the pros and cons of each possibility?
- What are the logical consequences of each possibility?
- What is the cost of each?
- What is the consequence of not acting?

Feeling

- How much do I care about what I gain or lose in each alternative?
- How will the people concerned react to the outcome?
- Will the outcome contribute to individual or group harmony?

The Challenge of Change in Organizations — summary notes

What extraverts and introverts need during times of change

Extraverts	Introverts
☐ Time to talk about what is going on	☐ Time alone to reflect on what is going on
☐ Involvement — something to do	☐ To be asked what they think about things
☐ Communication! Lots of it!	☐ Thought-out, written communication and one-on-one discussions
☐ To be heard and paid attention to; to have a voice	☐ Time to think through positions before discussions or meetings
☐ Action, getting on it, keeping up the pace	☐ Time to assimilate changes before taking action

What sensors and intuitors need during times of change

Sensors	Intuitors
☐ Real data — why is change occurring?	☐ The overall rationale
☐ Specifics and details about the changes	☐ A general plan to mentally play around with
☐ Connections between the changes and the past	☐ The chance to paint a picture of the future
☐ Realistic pictures of the future that make the changes real	☐ Options — a general direction, but not too much structure
☐ Clear guidelines on expectations, roles, and responsibilities, or the opportunity to design them	☐ The opportunity to participate in designing the future

What thinkers and feelers need during times of change

Thinkers	Feelers
☐ The logic behind the change	☐ Recognition of the impact of change on people
☐ What systemic change will there be? Why?	☐ How will people's needs be dealt with?
☐ Clarity in decision making and planning of change	☐ Inclusion of themselves and others
☐ What are the goals? What will be the structure?	☐ What values underlie the changes? Are they the right ones?
☐ Demonstration that leadership is competent	☐ Demonstration that leadership cares
☐ Fairness/equitability in the changes	☐ Appreciation and support

What judgers and perceivers need during times of change

Judgers	Perceivers
☐ A clear and concise plan of action	☐ An open-ended plan
☐ Defined outcomes, clear goals	☐ The general parameters
☐ A time frame with each stage spelled out	☐ Flexibility, with lots of options to choose from
☐ A clear statement of priorities	☐ Information and the opportunity to gather more
☐ No more surprises	☐ Loosen up — don't panic, trust the process
☐ Completion; get the changes in place	☐ Room to adjust as they go along

These summary notes are from the book "The Challenge of Change in Organizations" by Nancy Barger and Linda Kirby. Please be mindful and respectful of their use, using them for research or personal use only. Do not photocopy or distribute en masse, please!

Document in PowerPoint Slide Show - [Refocus and Renew for Managers vpublic3.ppt]

LIVE IT OUT

• If you do not already know it, determine your own personality type using the MBTI.

• Invite staff and key lay leaders to do the same and then discuss how your different personalities complement the way you work together.

CHAPTER 8
OVERCOMING RESISTANCES AND BARRIERS

While people present resistances and barriers to change externally, internally they are dealing with many emotions. It is wise to consider these emotions as we address resistances and barriers.

These change-driven emotions include:
- Shock and Fear
    People shut down rationally and survival emotions take over.
- Denial
    People ask what's wrong with the past and the way things are currently done. They deny the need to change.
- Loss and Sadness
    Traditions and memories have great meaning to some people. They see change as a significant loss.
- Anxiety and Disorientation
    People have understood their role in the way things are currently done. They feel inadequate in their new roles, or they don't see a role for themselves in the new way of doing things.

- Anger and Betrayal
    People devoted themselves to a purpose and identity (vision) that is changing. Some or all of their previous contributions might be viewed as worthless.
- Lethargy
    All the above emotions might snowball into lethargy and withdrawal from normal church activities.

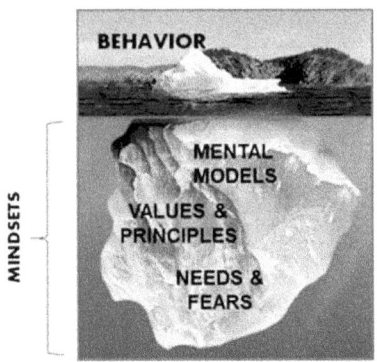

Recall the iceberg that represents our personal culture:

The internal emotions are well below the water line and manifest themselves in behaviors that present resistances and barriers.

Many of you may be saying that, the previous chapters are well and good, but I have resistances and barriers that prevent me/us from transforming our culture. Besides, I like to be liked by everyone. I'm the one that calms the seas, not rocks the boat.

In order to lead the transformation, you will have to rock the boat. You must create disequilibrium to achieve the threshold of change: The waves you and your team create will produce conflict, resistance, and barriers. You will learn how much disequilibrium you can create before reaching the limit of tolerance. Beyond the limit of tolerance, chaos and rebellion begin to appear.

This chapter is about how to address resistance and barriers, both the external ones and the internal ones. Let's start with the internal resistances and barriers.

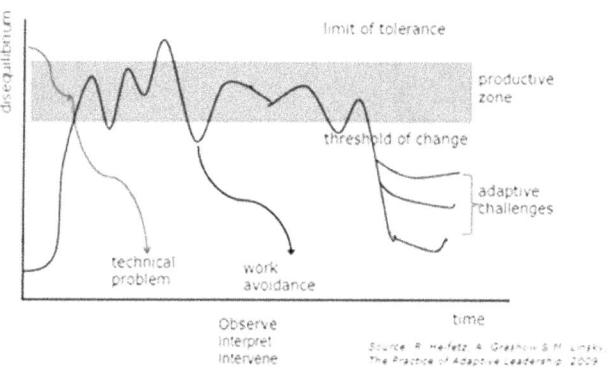

Resistances and Barriers (within Oneself)

We have been greatly helped by Gil Rendle's book Quietly Courageous, Leading the Church in a Changing World. Gil addresses three myths and three temptations that hinder our own sense of leadership. Gil says that quietly courageous leadership is about taking the next steps even when the final destination remains hidden.

- The first myth is that we live in a world of limited resources.
- The second myth is that rewards, organization and democratic decision making help the organization.
- The third myth is that additional learning (DMin, e.g.) will make a more effective leader.
- The first temptation is playing it safe.
- The second temptation is Christian empathy.
- The third temptation is to work harder and show commitment with tiredness.

We highly recommend his book, excerpts from which can be found later in this chapter.

External Resistances and Barriers

There are many articles and books written about dealing with resistances and barriers – particularly the tactics. Resistances and barriers create conflict when change actually begins to take place. The faster the change, the greater the potential for conflict. Responses to conflict are:

- Avoidance – many people would rather avoid conflict than face it.

- Smoothing - people agree to cosmetic changes that really change little while maintaining relationships.

- Fighting – this is a competitive win-lose approach which usually doesn't expose the root of the conflict (values, fears, needs, etc.)

- Compromise – everyone gets a little and everyone loses a little with little change. This is smoothing with the loss/weakening of relationships.

- Divorce – "I'm taking my ball and going home".

- Reconciling to a higher purpose & identity – people change their mindsets and behavior as they see an identity and purpose that changes lives.

The behavior that individual mindsets create are anger, frustration, snap conclusions from fear, loss of worth/power, etc.

Overall, in transformations, conflict is good. Let us repeat that, conflict is good. It means the person CARES about the change. It is important to understand why they care.

Value of Conflict & Responses to Conflict

The value of conflict is:

- The person raising barriers really cares
- Danger of Too Much Agreement
    - critical information may be withheld
    - pros and cons not carefully considered
    - failure to collect data that clarifies the team's decision(s)
    - may not be tested against reality
    - diversity of ideas discouraged, reducing buy-in and carry through

To view conflict as positive, you must believe the following:
- Conflict is natural and can be valuable
- Conflict can be a source of energy
- Conflict is the result of real differences
- Different perspectives are often necessary for breakthrough thinking
- The leader's views and habits in handling conflict are important determinants of the outcomes of a conflict
- Mastering skills in managing conflict takes lots of practice

In assessing your response to conflict, ask yourself two questions:
- How important to you is the opinion, goal, or perspective under discussion?
- How important to you is it to maintain good relationships with the people with whom you are in conflict?

Common responses to conflict include:
- Avoiding the conflict
- Smoothing over the conflict
- Escalating the conflict to force win/lose outcomes
- Compromising the solution
- Problem solving through the conflict

Problem solving through the conflict process:
- What is the overarching goal that this effort supports?
- Write down the problem that is being solved.
- Present each idea and comment/ask questions only for clarity.
- Then, discuss each in terms of short-term impact, impact on other parts of the organization, long-term implications and practicality (availability of people and money).

- One person speaks at a time.

- Seek a solution that solves the problem and that everyone can support. It does not have to be everyone's first choice.

Tactics for Conflict Intervention

- select neutral territory
- make sure the setting is informal
- make sure all the appropriate people are present
- set an agenda and ground rules; stick to them
- manage the time carefully
- use active listening and constructive feedback skills throughout the intervention

One approach to dealing with the resistances and barriers that cause conflict is to focus on two things: 1) the purpose & identity that the church is aspiring to and 2) understanding and addressing the mindsets that lead to resistance and the erection of barriers. We have previously discussed Purpose & Identity and how it must permeate every aspect of church activity.

Understanding mindsets that create the behavioral response requires:
- Discussing the values, fears, and basic needs that the individual sees for himself/herself AND for the faith community.
- Authentically listening, not simply preparing for a rebuttal.
- Understanding the assumptions behind these perspectives.
- Acknowledging loss as well as historic contributions

Reconciling perspective and feelings requires:
- Clear destination of the Purpose & Identity
- Reason(s) for the Change
- Description of the Alternatives considered.

- The Payoff of the Change
- The Cost of the Change

Asking how the resistance or barrier would impede the progress towards God's intent for your church.

Never use email for this reconciliation. It requires telephone, conferencing (Zoom, FaceTime, Duo, etc) or face-to-face meeting(s).

In the next section you will find useful perspectives on Respectful Contrary (a dialogue tool about conflict that Ted values), Guidelines for Responding to Group Problems, and Layers of Resistance as you may encounter them.

Biblical Illiteracy as a Barrier

One of the great barriers for many denominations is the Biblical illiteracy of its members. For many, their Biblical knowledge is limited to a twenty minute sermon each Sunday (with today's average Sunday attendance twice per month) which are repeated every three years. The Bible is so much richer than that. Ted's own experience is that his Biblical knowledge gained over that last six years far outweighs his knowledge gained over the previous sixty years.

Intentional discipleship is necessary for people to change their idols to the Identity & Purpose discerned for your local church. The issues discussed in the New Testament by Paul are familiar to today's church, for example Corinth and Ephesus. Study of the Word is fundamental to a shift in culture; your leadership is ineffective without it.

LIVE IT OUT

- Honestly identify your own areas of resistance to change.
- Engage those whom you disagree with and use the Respectful Contrary (discussed in tools) to gain better understanding of their perspective.

CHAPTER 8
OVERCOMING RESISTANCES AND BARRIERS
TOOLS

Many of us are stymied by the roadblocks of resistance and barriers. These tools help leaders to overcome them.

- Resistances and Barriers within Oneself
- Respectful Contrary – Responding to One-to-One Problems
- Guidelines for Responding to Group Problems

The prayer and scripture are offered for spiritual grounding as you use these tools.

PRAYER

Gracious God, you love us in spite of our tendency to reject and resist your love. Give us the same capacity to love unconditionally and to regard those who oppose our ideas as brothers and sisters who love you no less than we do. Open our ears and minds to truly hear their concerns and fears, and open our hearts to respond in ways that reflect your love and grace so that we might together build up the body of Christ. In his precious name we pray. Amen.

SCRIPTURE

"Therefore, if you are offering your gift at the altar and there remember that your brother or sister has something against you, leave your gift there in front of the altar. First go and be reconciled to them; then come and offer your gift."

John 13:34-35

RESISTANCES AND BARRIERS WITHIN ONESELF

A summary of Gil Rendle's book

In this segment, we will summarize our key learnings about Gil Rendle's book Quietly Courageous, Leading the Church in a Changing World. Gil has given us permission to summarize his book.

Gil addresses three myths and three temptations that hinder our own sense of leadership. Gil says that quietly courageous leadership is about taking the next steps even when the final destination remains hidden. We highly recommend his book.

A Word about Enough

- There is a myth that we live in a world of limited resources.

- Additive decision making is a process by which we add a good idea to the list without taking anything off. Additive decision making increases the complexity of congregational and denominational structures as each new issue or group is given a committee and budget.

- Breaking the addiction of additive decision making requires making choices, choosing yes for only the most important and no for all others. Such choices can be made only when the leader has first helped the people shape and form themselves around a purpose.

- Power is misunderstood as confined within our institutions and their leaders. God's power can be found in many faithful people.

- Non-profits need to shift their measurements to outcomes and away from resources and activities. How many churches do not give high priority to confessions of faith and lives impacted in the community but do measure worship attendance and finances?[54]

A Word about Structure and Processes

- This chapter addresses assumptions about fear, organization and democracy. These practices have been strengths well used in the past but are increasingly becoming weaknesses.

Fear

- Courage needs to be redefined as a choice to be made rather than a feeling to be controlled. It is less the response of the stirred heart than of the discerning mind.

- Fear of the reward system occurs when the terms of employment set by the very people led is a constraint on leadership. Fear occurs when the pastor's performance is measured by how satisfied members are with their own congregational experience as opposed to whether ministry outcomes are produced

---

[54]Summary notes of Chapter 4 - Rendle, Gil, Quietly Courageous: Leading the Church in a Changing World, Lanham, MD: Rowman & Littlefield, 2019.

- Leading without regard for reward is what Moses and Aaron faced when the whole Israelite community complained after only forty-five days of liberation from slavery (Exodus 16:2)

Structure
- Most of current congregational and denominational structures are hierarchical, linear and bureaucratically organized.
- Bishop Robert Schnase of The United Methodist Church stated, "We began to treat congregations, districts and conferences like interconnected widgets that must operate in uniform fashion or else the connections will suffer.... Context didn't matter. Unity relied upon common structures more than a common sense of mission."
- The top of the organization is actually the most distant from the change that needs to be addressed. Decision making and learning must happen at the edge, where institutions encounter the liquid culture.
- Ideology is the glue that holds (decentralized) organizations together. The means and practices by which one gets from identity and purpose to real results is agile, and at times chaotic, and will ultimately help organizations learn what to do next.

Democracy
- Courageous leaders need to know to fear the absence of discernment and clear decisions more than they fear critique and criticism for changing familiar ways.
- Representation and egalitarianism are practices that go back to the founding of our country and the Methodist Church.
- Representation within the church is not to measure the greatest passions within parts of the congregation, denomination or institution but to discern the most faithful path for the whole body.
- The assumption of egalitarianism is that all congregations should be treated equally. Leaders in the current divergent landscape must be much more discerning to follow the actual definition of egalitarianism as an equality of rights and opportunities, not an equality of treatment.

- Egalitarianism practiced as fairness paradoxically requires leaders to focus 80 percent of their time, attention, and resources on the 20 percent of the system that demonstrates recalcitrance, weakness, inability and disinterest.[55]

A Word about Learning

- Placeholder clergy have the basic skills in the core functions of preaching, pastoral care, and sacramental ministry but have not developed the capacities for effective leadership of congregations. Conflict averse and unclear about the nature of human systems and organizations, talented but tenuous clergy wait for permission to lead.

- The Dreyfus model of professional development:

    - Novice – Learning the Rules of the Game (theory)
    - Advanced Beginner – Using Rules in Context (competence)
    - Competent to Proficient – The Intuitive Leap (acting intuitively)
    - Expertise (thinking intuitively)
    - Mastery (using multiple disciplines and continuously learning)

- Clergy professional peer groups are, perhaps, the best example of communities of practice available to clergy. Consultants, mentors, coaches, and spiritual directors are all avenues that clergy can use to make their work and life transparent to themselves; hold their work up to current knowledge, standards, and peer review; and receive feedback with support and accountability. However, clergy professional peer groups (in which participants intentionally choose to participate, as opposed to being required or assigned by their denomination) appear to be the richest opportunity for learning and continued development of professional mastery.[56]

---

[55] Summary notes of Chapter 5 - Rendle, Gil, Quietly Courageous: Leading the Church in a Changing World, Lanham, MD: Rowman & Littlefield, 2019.

[56] Summary notes of Chapter 6 - Rendle, Gil, Quietly Courageous: Leading the Church in a Changing World, Lanham, MD: Rowman & Littlefield, 2019.

The Temptation of Playing It Safe

- Leaders must be able to shape a vision and outcomes for the future without being sure of their own direction.

- Nostalgia invites us into a one-sided story. An unknown future, coupled with the anxiety of the present, makes the nostalgic past a grand temptation.

- Nostalgia invites us to rely on the past diagnosis. Nostalgia carries the temptation to work harder at what we already know how-to-do in order to recapture a time and strength that no longer exist.

- Nostalgia invites us to avoid difficult questions. Organization defensive culture prevents individuals or segments of the organization from experiencing embarrassment or threat.

- "Playing It Safe" creates the life cycle of a congregation that goes from visioning to structure to ministry to nostalgia to polarity to death.[57]

The Temptation of Christian Empathy

- The Christian New Testament law of love is the fundamental discipline of caring for the other. Empathy is a Christian good, shared in some form with all religions.

- Empathy in leadership was never meant to be a deterrent to action.

- Unchecked empathy favors relationship over purpose.

- Unchecked empathy favors weakness over strength. (Or over attention to stress and discomfort)

- Empathy holds leaders hostage to the "client in the room".

- The more the leader can verbalize and demonstrate purpose in a stressed system, the more the people will mirror the attention of the leader. People over time increase their attention to that which the leader gives his or her primary attention.

- The discomfort of the current time can be eclipsed by a mission future. [58]

---

[57] Summary notes of Chapter 7 - Rendle, Gil, Quietly Courageous: Leading the Church in a Changing World, Lanham, MD: Rowman & Littlefield, 2019.

The Temptation of Tiredness

- Tiredness is tempting because it is another of those aspects of leadership that is highly rewarded. Being able to log eighty or more hours a week laboring at leadership is often perceived as heroic and as a demonstrable sacrifice in the eyes of many.

- Running harder to stay in place (i.e. the Alice in Wonderland effect)
  - We are too much a part of the culture to let go of old assumptions.
  - We are unaware of alternatives.
  - We follow policies and procedures to avoid embarrassment or threat

- Mission statements are aspirational; the aspiration invites tiredness to the point of exhaustion. [note: Identity and Purpose are directional].

- Surplus powerlessness is the set of feelings and beliefs that make people think of themselves as even more powerless than the actual power situation requires, and then leaves them to act in ways that actually confirm them in their powerlessness. (Jim Collins, Good to Great in the Social Sector)

- Surplus powerlessness certainly constrains clergy from pursuing accountability for practices of discipleship in the lives of congregants. It constrains congregations from developing credible strategies for making their communities healthier and less assaulted by drugs, violence or the breakdown of family structures.

- Grand, ultimate aspirations can so cause overwhelm that leaders will plan modest and meager efforts [below the threshold of change] that will quite naturally fail, knowing that failure will just affirm again how important and difficult their aspiration is and how noble it was for them to have tried.[59]

---

[58]Summary notes of Chapter 8 - Rendle, Gil, Quietly Courageous: Leading the Church in a Changing World, Lanham, MD: Rowman & Littlefield, 2019.

[59]Summary notes of Chapter 9 - Rendle, Gil, Quietly Courageous: Leading the Church in a Changing World, Lanham, MD: Rowman & Littlefield, 2019.

RESPECTFUL CONTRARY[60]

Guidelines for Responding to One-to-One Problem

Respectful Contrary is one means to heal strained relationships, strengthen bonds, build trust and clarify issues.

Reality seems to be like a diamond, and everyone stands on a different facet of it. What others see or understand may differ dramatically from what I see and understand. We can only tell what we see and listen to the perspectives of others with interest.

Contrary (first person)
1. When you do _____ (describe the behavior operationally)
2. I (make myself) feel _____ (some version of mad, sad, glad or scared)
3. What I want from you is _____ (again, descriptive language)
4. If the same thing happens again, let's do this: _____

Response to the Contrary (second person)
1. I heard you say _____ (repeat their meaning in your own words. Allow corrections)
2. I think that means _____ (give your interpretation)
3. The way I feel about feeling that is _____ (this is an important part, a second layer)

Repeat as often as necessary.

---

[60]Corporate Potential, St. Paul, MN 1987

Guidelines for Responding to One-to-One Problem
- Anticipate and prevent problems whenever possible.
    - know each other
    - establish ground rules
    - discuss norms for group behavior
- Work hard to understand where the person is coming from
- Think of each problem as a group problem
- Neither overreact nor underreact
    - do nothing during the conflict; ask for prayer
    - off-line conversation
    - impersonal group time; self-examine group process
    - off-line confrontation; contract with group leader
    - in-group confrontation
    - expulsion from the group (rare)

TEN COMMON GROUP PROBLEMS[61]

1. Floundering
characteristics
- false starts, directionless discussions and activities
- postponed decisions

corrective actions
- review the mission
- review the problem statement
- review the plan
- identify the barriers
- unspoken disagreement on the next step

---

[61]The Team Handbook by Peter R. Scholtes, Joiner Associates, Madison, WI, 1988

2. Overbearing Participants
characteristics
- discourages or forbids discussion in their "area of expertise"
- discounts any proposed activity by declaring that it won't work.

corrective actions
- reinforce ground rules
- get the overbearing participant (before the meeting or project) to agree that it is important for all of the team members to be involved and to be heard. Ask for their patience.
- enforce the primacy of data and target audience input.

3. Dominating Participants
characteristics
- consumes disproportionate amount of air-time
- long anecdotes
- moments of silence are invitation for the dominator to talk
- inhibits teamwork, members get discouraged and find excuses to miss meetings.

corrective actions
- structure discussion on key issues to encourage equal participation (post-it notes, written summaries before speaking with timelines)
- critique meetings is terms of balance of participation; ensure ground-rules include balanced participation, time limits and focused discussion
- practice gatekeeping ("Joe, thanks for your input. _____, what is your perspective?")

4. Reluctant Participants
characteristics
- "I am participating by listening. When I have something to say, I'll speak up."

corrective actions
- structure discussion on key issues to encourage equal participation (post-it notes, written summaries before speaking with timelines)
- divide tasks into individual assignments and reports
- practice gatekeeping ("Joe, _____, what is your perspective?" or looking directly at the reluctant participant, ask "Does anyone else have ideas about this?")

5. Unquestioned Acceptance of Opinions as Facts
characteristics
- self-assured statements of personal beliefs and assumptions

corrective actions
- "Do you have some data or references that we could study further to understand your point?"
- "Do others share this view?"
- "How can we validate this perspective with our church?"

6. Rush to Accomplishment
characteristics
- Individual reaches an individual decision about a problem and its solution before the group has had time to understand the problem and consider different options
- Their nonverbal behavior, direct statements and "throw away" expressions constantly communicate impatience.

corrective actions
- Follow the approach of define the problem, gather data, analyze the options, select an improvement plan, gain consensus from others if applicable, and implement with standardized work.
- Make sure you, as the leader, are not the source of the problem.
- Work with the rusher to project the impact hasty decisions without buy-in.

7. Attribution
characteristics
- We tend to attribute motives to people (or other teams) when we disagree with or don't understand their opinion, Through attribution we try to bring order and meaning into apparent disorder and confusion.
- It creates resentment when someone else tells you that they know what makes you tick or tries to explain your motives.

corrective actions
- for individuals, use the Respectful Contrary
- for teams:
  - understand their mission and the implications of the solution with their goals
  - revisit problem definition and the scope of data gathering (did we get a broad enough sampling)

8. Discounts and "Plops"
characteristics
- When someone ignores or discounts my value or perspective, I feel discounted.
- Being discounted can cause hostility

corrective actions
- train the team on active listening
- support the discounted by asking them to clarify their statement. "Nancy made a valid point. Nancy, would you restate your thought."
- work off-line with anyone who frequently discounts or ignores other's statements.

9. Wanderlust: Digression and Tangents
characteristics
- straying from the subject to "pontificate" about a subject or to tell a story
- straying from the subject to avoid a sensitive topic

corrective actions

- Use written agenda with estimated times for each item.

- Direct the conversation back on track.

- Capture digressions on a "bucket list" chart and review as part of future agendas.

10. Feuding Team Members

characteristics

- Argue for the sake of winning the argument, not solving the issue

corrective actions

- Be careful about member selection for a team.

- Bring the two people together before the first meeting to work out an agreement about their behavior.

- If confrontation occurs during a meeting, get the adversaries to discuss the issue off-line with a facilitator

CHAPTER 9
CARING FOR LEADERS

Leading change is hard work that demands deep wells of spiritual, emotional, mental and physical energy in order to avoid depression and burnout. So it is important for leaders, both pastors and laity, to engage in activities and practices that feed body, mind and spirit.

More than ever today, leaders are feeling higher demands and fewer rewards. As Alan Nelson observes, "The cost of effective leadership is high, but there is the perception that, especially in the church, the rewards often do not outweigh the costs."[62] Such a drain can be disabling without adequate self-care.

We have found that many leaders feel guilty about committing adequate time to self-care. It cannot be stressed too strongly, though, that self-care is not selfish. It benefits both the leader and those the leader seeks to serve. An empty "tank" provides no help when sharing oneself with others.

---

[62]Nelson, Alan E., Leading Your Ministry, Nashville, Abingdon Press, 1996, 22

Nurturing the Leader's Spirit

Most critical for those seeking to lead culture change in congregations is paying attention to the leader's own spirit. J. Oswald Sanders advises that, "Spiritual leadership requires Spirit-filled people. Other qualities are important; to be Spirit-filled is indispensable."[63] Some have referred to the importance of constructing a "wall of spirituality" that will withstand resistance and attacks from those who would sabotage change efforts. Lewis Parks and Bruce Birch call for "a robust intimacy with God" as an essential tool for leaders in the church.[64]

Personal spiritual disciplines represent the foundation for the wall of spirituality. Prayer, Bible reading, acts of service, fasting and meditation can all be helpful tools that feed the leader's spirit. We have found that tithing and generous giving of financial resources also enhances and feeds. It is truly more blessed to give than to receive, and the blessings are at least as much to the giver as to those who receive.

Personal spirituality is also a matter of integrity, given that others will not follow where leaders are not willing to go. Developing a strong spiritual life not only benefits the leader, but models a pattern that creates an environment more conducive to change and growth in discipleship throughout the congregation.

Perhaps it should go without saying (but we want to emphasize it anyway) that worship is essential for leaders. Finding adequate opportunities to worship can be especially challenging for pastoral leaders who are tasked with leading worship on a regular basis. We've known our share of pastors who claim to worship while the choir is singing or scripture is being read (by others presumably). But this limited type of worship is insufficient. Those who lead worship "professionally" must find other means to worship personally. With the proliferation of online worship this has become much easier, especially when many services are recorded and available on demand. Andy found worship at local monastic communities gratifying and nourishing for his soul.

---

[63]Sanders, J Oswald, Spiritual Leadership: Principles of Excellence for Every Believer, 79

[64]Lewis Parks & Bruce Birch, Ducking Spears, Dancing Madly, Nashville, Abingdon Press, 2004, 112.

In our experience, even those with no responsibility for leading worship need more than a single weekly service. Whether in small groups, online, or at midweek services offered by other churches, additional worship can be extremely helpful for all leaders.

Relationships offer a primary role in feeding one's spirit. While leading change demands the commitment of large amounts of time, it should not excuse efforts to cultivate personal relationships with family, friends, and colleagues. Many well-intentioned pastors in particular have been known to sacrifice family at the altar of their ministry. Regular date nights with a spouse, participating in sports or other activities with children, and frequent family times fuel loving relationships that in turn feed the leader's spirit.

Sabbath may seem to some an outdated term and even more outdated concept. But we find regular Sabbath days to be critical for all leaders. Sabbath time provides renewal re-creation, and rest that are not available from any other source. It is crucial to understand that Sabbath is not simply ceasing one's work. While tempting to use so-called Sabbath time to catch up on household chores, this does not provide the needed rest and renewal that true Sabbath can offer. Perhaps the best way to understand Sabbath is time to devote to activities that feed our spiritual selves. So much of ministry and leadership is draining and Sabbath offers the opportunity to replenish and restore energy for our spirits.

These are all options for feeding the leader's spirit, but each individual will need to discover and practice those habits that are most nourishing for them. Herb Miller, in "Leadership is the Key," points to four distinct kinds of spiritual food that relate to personality types and advises:

> *If the spiritual food you receive and serve each day in your ministry role does not match your spiritual type, the incompatibility will register itself in feelings of emptiness, frustration or anger.*[65]

---

[65] Herb Miller, Leadership is the Key: Unlocking Your Ministry Effectiveness, Nashville, Abingdon Press,1997,42

Nurturing the Leader's Mind

Regular reading and study, especially about theology and leadership concepts helps to nurture the leader's mind. But one should really make room for all kinds of reading—including current events and fiction. These keep the mind open to learning new things, as well as being exposed to new perspectives that otherwise might be missed.

Continuing education and training events sponsored by denominational and other Christian sources can offer invaluable help to those working to change culture in congregations. Reading this book, for example, will enhance the leader's understanding and ability for the leadership role. Parks and Birch cite theologian Paul Tillich in holding up the need for "a robust correlation of scripture and theology with the best thinking in secular leadership studies."[66]

Likewise, keeping in touch with culture and media will assist in relating to members of the congregation and community. It enables the leader to remain up to date on current issues and perspectives. Pastors, in particular, can often fall prey to spending all of their time in a church environment and easily lose touch with experiences and thoughts of the surrounding community. Many pastors have been known to proudly proclaim that they watch little if any television. We view this as irresponsible behavior since it severely limits awareness of popular culture that is influencing the thoughts and actions of those in the congregation and community.

Intentional interaction through pastoral encounters and social engagements also helps leaders to keep in touch with those they serve and seek to lead. An old farmer in one of Andy's congregations was fond of saying in planning meetings that, "the dog food's only as good as the dogs will eat." Andy understood this to mean that many plans and strategies fail because they don't connect with people's context and perceived needs. Personal interaction helps to frame and shape change efforts in ways that are more likely to be accepted.

---

[66] Lewis Parks & Bruce Birch, Ducking Spears, Dancing Madly, Nashville, Abingdon Press, 2004, 22.

Nurturing the Leader's Body

Leading change, as we've said before, is hard, demanding work that taxes spirit, mind and body. Many leaders, either intentionally or accidentally, ignore or avoid the need to adequately care for physical needs. This avoidance is harmful, both to the leader and to those being served. Care of the body is basically a theological decision to honor that which is created in the image of God.

Perhaps the most lacking aspect of self-care today is finding adequate rest. "Burning the candle at both ends" is regarded as a badge of honor in many circles. Insomnia is widespread, as is the use of caffeine and other stimulants to make up for inadequate sleep. While we have emphasized the importance of Sabbath rest to the spirit's nourishment, it is no less important for the body. Like long daily hours, not taking full advantage of vacation time is honored in a competitive society. The wise leader will both observe a weekly sabbath and take all allotted vacation time.

Bill Hybels, in his book, "Courageous Leadership," relates his own personal crisis that led him to conclude that The pace at which I've been doing the work of God is destroying God's work in me. Subsequently, while he was engaging in therapy Hybels' counselor suggested that he reflect on all the forms of recreation he was involved in and determine which was most restorative. Bill's response was, "that doesn't require reflection. That's easy, I don't do anything for recreation." "After getting over his shock," Hybels relates, "my counselor simply said, 'Bill, you'd better start. Immediately.'"[67]

This is wise advice for any leader.

Busy schedules frequently contribute to poor nutritional habits. Grabbing coffee and donuts for breakfast and fast food for lunch are common patterns for many. But neither is conducive to good health and nutrition. There is good reason that pastors today are ranked among the most at risk professions by insurance

---

[67] Bill Hybels, Courageous Leadership, Grand Rapids, Zondervan, 2009, 244

companies, largely due to poor nutrition and obesity. Nurturing the body begins with providing adequate and healthy fuel.

In a similar vein, many pastors claim to be too busy for regular physical activity. Numerous studies have documented the importance of being active to overall health and longevity. Long hours in a gym are not essential, but building time for walking or other physical activity is. The human body is designed for movement and suffers if it does not occur.

Certainly, some will want to argue that advice such as this represents an intrusion on personal space and individual liberty. On the contrary, we would claim that caring for the leader's spiritual, mental and physical well-being is essential for long term ministry and leadership. Both the individual leader and the congregation (not to mention the leader's family) suffer if there is not adequate attention to self-care as described above.

Leading at the Edge of Chaos

Leading change is unpredictable, often messy, and chaotic. Yet, as Margaret Wheatley cautions, "In order to thrive in a world of change and chaos, we will need to accept chaos as an essential process by which natural systems, including organizations, renew and revitalize themselves."[68]

Edwin Friedman, based on his study of family systems, claims that in times of crisis the single variable that distinguished those who survived and flourished from those that disintegrated was what he called a well-differentiated leader.

> I mean someone who has clarity about his or her own life goals, and, therefore, someone who is less likely to become lost in the anxious emotional processes swirling about. I mean someone who can be separate while still remaining connected, and therefore can maintain a modifying

---

[68]Wheatley, Margaret, Leadership and the New Science: Discovering Order in a Chaotic World, Berrett-Koehler Publishing, San Francisco, CA, 2006

non-anxious, and sometimes challenging process. I mean someone who can manage his or her own reactivity to the automatic reactivity of others, and therefore be able to take stands at the risk of displeasing. It is not as though some leaders can do this and some cannot. No one does this easily, and most leaders, I have learned, can improve their capacity.[69]

How leaders respond to chaos is the key. When leaders take a reactive stance, change becomes even more messy and chaotic. While there is always a need for adaptive leadership that responds to emerging needs and contexts, wise leaders will act proactively in those areas where it is possible. Certainly, personal care is one of those areas that can serve as an anchor in a sea of chaos.

LIVE IT OUT

- Create a plan to assure and care for your own spiritual, mental, emotional and physical well-being.

---

[69] Friedman, Edwin H., A Failure of Nerve: Leadership in the Age of the Quick Fix – 10th Edition, 14

CHAPTER 9
CARING FOR LEADERS
TOOLS

- Nurturing the Leader's Spirit
- Nurturing the Leader's Mind
- Nurturing the Leader's Body

The prayer and scripture are offered for spiritual grounding as you use these tools.

PRAYER

Understanding God, living a life of service and seeking to lead others is hard work that often leaves us exhausted and frustrated. Lead us to green pastures where we might find rest. Help us to discover paths that lead to refreshment and renewal and to activities that feed our spirit. By the power of the Holy Spirit fill us with renewed energy and purpose for doing your will for the sake of Jesus Christ our Savior and Lord. Amen.

SCRIPTURE

"Do you not know that your bodies are temples of the Holy Spirit, who is in you, whom you have received from God? You are not your own; you were bought at a price. Therefore honor God with your bodies"

1 Corinthians 6:19-20

Nurturing the Leader's Spirit

• Spiritual Disciplines – Find and use a devotional guide that best suits your stage in faith. Andy uses the Upper Room Disciplines which follow the Common Lectionary with daily scripture, interpretation and prayer. Set aside a time, preferably at the beginning or ending of the day for a time of personal reflection and prayer. Practice personal disciplines such as breath prayer (repeating words of scripture or a hymn in rhythm with breathing in and out), journaling, fasting, etc.

• Worship – Set aside a time each week for your own worship. If you are a pastor or worship leader this cannot be during regular weekly worship. Find a nearby church that offers mid-week worship or a local monastery or retreat center that welcomes visitors.

• Sabbath – Choose an entire 24-hour period during which you endeavor to do no work, unless it is mowing the lawn (Andy's habit) or anything else that feeds your spirit. Read, listen to music, walk in the woods, pray, do whatever feeds you because the other six days will deplete your spiritual and emotional energy. Jewish rabbi's even suggest the Sabbath can be a time for intimate relationships with a spouse. The point is, use your Sabbath to fuel your spirit so that you have enough to lead others the rest of the week.

• Relationships – It is not unusual for those engaged in leading ministry (both clergy and laity) to do so at the expense of relationships with family and friends. We rationalize that doing the Lord's work is more important: how can serving God be bad? But all too often our family, in particular, pays the unintended price for our ministry. Keep regular date nights with a spouse, make time to spend with children—attend their concerts, sports events and recitals—and keep in touch with close friends in intentional ways. You can always put these events on your calendar and then you can simply say, "I have an appointment at that time."

• Renewal – We frequently hear people boast of not taking all their vacation time or never taking a sick day. Our experience indicates this is unhealthy. Renewal comes through times of recreation and rest.

Nurturing the Leader's Mind

• Reading and Study – It is important to read beyond the required professional reading. Find an author whose novels you enjoy; explore biographies of people you admire. Read several newspapers (probably online today) to provide varying perspectives.

• Continuing Education – Many of us use continuing education to learn more about things we already enjoy and do well. Take an honest assessment (or better yet, ask your colleagues) of areas where you could do better and focus continuing education on those areas.

• Relating to popular culture and media – Especially for preachers it is not constructive to say, "I never watch television." Watching televised dramas, listening to contemporary music, and catching an occasional movie are all ways to keep in touch with those you serve and the world that shapes their opinions and actions.

• "Enough" pastoral encounters – If you follow our suggestions for empowering laity to do pastoral ministry you may find yourself not making any visits. This is overshooting the mark. Again, this is a way of keeping in touch with the needs, fears and anxieties of the people we serve. If you are a pastor, perhaps you would want to be the one to provide pastoral care to key leaders. The point is to stay in touch.

• Networking – Find other congregations who are facing similar challenges and intentionally reach out to them. Include colleagues and friends in other denominations from whom we can learn much.

Nurturing the Leader's Body

- Adequate rest – Authorities indicate we need seven to nine hours of sleep each night. Burning the candle at both ends should not be seen as a badge of honor. Eventually it will wear on the most hardy of us. The widespread prevalence of burnout is very often the result of inadequate rest (as well as failure to pay attention to the needs of the leader's spirit mentioned above.

- Nutrition - Pastors, in particular, have become one of the highest risk occupations in insurance mortality tables, largely because of obesity. We don't recommend rigid diets; rather strive for eating regular and balanced meals. Pay attention to what you put into your body and consider that you are providing fuel for the marathon of ministry.

- Exercise – If going to the gym, playing tennis or pickle ball are your thing, great! But everyone can benefit from simple exercise like walking. Even 15 minutes of walking produces proven health benefits. Tai Chi and Yoga also provide both physical and mental benefits. Find what best fits into your schedule and keep regular exercise.

- Pay attention to the use of stimulants & other substances – We're not talking about illegal drugs (though we've surely known our share of church leaders who have fallen into dependency) but rather encouraging moderation in the use of coffee, tea or alcohol.

CHAPTER 10
ENVISIONING A CHANGED CULTURE

In the midst of struggling to adapt to a changing world and with the inertia of years, or even decades, of doing things the same way, it might be hard to even envision what a changed congregational culture might look like. But we want to give you at least a glimpse of what a more vital culture for your congregation might be and hope for achieving it. With a renewed focus on commitment to Jesus Christ as Lord and the congregation's God-given purpose, the church is more likely to resemble the dynamic original Christian movement (often referred to as "the way") rather than an entrenched and static institution.

A changed culture depends on making a number of key paradigm shifts. A paradigm shift, which is a concept identified by the American physicist and philosopher Thomas Kuhn,[70] is a fundamental change in the basic concepts and experimental practices of a scientific discipline. Even though Kuhn restricted the use of the term to the natural sciences, the concept of a paradigm shift has also been used in numerous non-scientific contexts to describe a profound change in a fundamental model or perception of events. Paradigms (a way of describing

---

[70] https://en.wikipedia.org/wiki/Paradigm_shift

culture) establish boundaries and provide the rules for success. They help people simplify the complex world, understand situations and make decisions.

While paradigms are helpful in living in a complex world, people tend to filter out information that doesn't fit the paradigm. Joel Barker (Future Edge, 1993)[71] said that people shoot down good ideas because they assume that the future is merely an extension of the past. Many things we accept today once met substantial resistance from thoughtful people. People resist change when they operate within old paradigms. Barker calls this the "Paradigm Effect." This effect can block creative solutions to problems and the ability to see the future.

Describing change in terms of paradigm shifts is a key ingredient in understanding the desired change and leading toward a new vision.

There are many paradigm shifts that you may desire for your church culture. We share some key shifts that we think will apply to most churches.

Programs & Building → **Church** → **Purpose & Identity**

1. We have already spoken about this shift, but it bears repeating. When the Purpose & Identity of the local church are unclear, people gravitate to concrete items like programs and building. More than simply a shift of focus, this involves a transformation in which a vision that represents Purpose & Identity drives behavior and decision making for the congregation. While many churches operate with multiple values and foci, only a focus on purpose & identity will move the congregation toward more vital ministry.

Programs and building are necessary elements for a church; undoubtedly, they are necessary for any non-profit organization. But they can become

---

[71]Now published as Barker, Joel Arthur, Paradigms: The Business of Discovering the Future, Harper Collins Publishers, New York, NY, 1992

idols, replacing God as the reason people come to church, and becoming the source of disagreements within the church when given the wrong priority.

All programs are good, but some are better in making disciples for Christ. In order to align programs with the purpose, it means that some programs can be suspended without devaluing the people who supported them; celebrate what they have done and how they contributed to the church and surrounding community. The energy for programs should come from members who feel called to serve.

Church-owned buildings are not necessary for a church; let us repeat, church-owned buildings are not necessary for a church. They are convenient for corporate worship, children's Christian learning, and social activities. Corporate worship can now take place with electronic connections; families can gather in the homes for worship and study; social activities can be arranged in other venues. **BUT, relationships are enhanced with the ability to meet in person.** Therefore, the long-term view about church buildings must be different from the last two centuries. Buildings should be adaptable and flexible to meet evolving church and community needs.

2. Inevitably, when a congregation commits to purpose as the primary driver, the congregation organizes for ministry in a different way. The move is one from siloed management to shared leadership—a partnership. As with so many other areas, this is a lesson churches can learn from observing business and industry (one of the reasons our partnership has been so fruitful).

The organization of a church and its denomination may reflect the organizational needs of decades past. Rigid requirements reflect a time of lower education, lower experience and slower communications. Rigid requirements also placed activity management into silos. Education opportunities also created professional pastors, whom the members regarded as "employees" who were paid to do the

Lord's work. It allowed laity to drift father and farther from serving the Lord because "that's what paid staff is to do". Laity must become stakeholders in their church and share leadership responsibilities for the goals and outcomes of the local church. Roles need to be redefined from membership to pastors.

A specific example is the chief "administrative" or "executive" committee of the church, which we will call the Church Council. It generally is staffed with the team/committee leaders of the church and the pastor(s). Committee reports often dominate this body's meeting. This Church Council's role should include alignment and integration of the ministries (teams and committees) to best meet the Purpose & Identity of the church. It can reduce the time devoted to committee reports by establishing a covenant with each ministry and written committee reports posted several days before the meeting. A second role is strategy – looking at how the efforts of all will fulfill what God is calling the church to do.

Returning to our image of the football field (forgive us, we're both aging athletes) many churches appear to have multiple teams on the field, each pursuing their own agenda (or game plan). The result is lots of activity (and plenty of exhausted, burned out "players") but little advancement toward the goal. In fact, it can be worse than that! Often each committee working to achieve its own goals can result in conflicts and collisions as they get in each other's way. They engage in competition for available resources of time, energy and funding.

Shared leadership, in contrast, unites all teams/committees in pursuing the common goal of the congregation's mission and purpose. It works in aligning resources of time, talent and finances toward that common purpose. The resulting achievements can then be celebrated by all and inspire continued shared leadership.

3. We believe it is essential for the pastor to shift from being a spiritual teacher to becoming a spiritual shepherd and leader. The roles are not mutually exclusive, but the one which takes priority influences the likelihood of shared ministry leading to vitality.

A spiritual teacher provides information, which is essential, but insufficient, for achieving change in congregational culture. When Andy taught preaching at Wesley Theological Seminary, he emphasized the importance of applying scripture to life, and not simply analyzing its meaning. The spiritual teacher puts information "out there," while the spiritual leader inspires people to put their learning into action in productive ways that lead more people to discipleship and provide more resources for ministry.

The spiritual shepherd may be content to maintain the status quo of the congregation, while the spiritual leader develops his/her flock in Christian discipleship. They work to sanctify the faith community toward individual fulfillment and corporate fulfillment of the Purpose & Identity that God calls for their church. The pastor continually asks others to test their thoughts and actions against that Purpose & Identity, as well as the fulfillment of the Great Commission (Matt. 28:19-20) and the Great Commandment (Matt. 22:37-40).

One of the challenges for most pastors is the desire to be liked. Trying to keep everyone happy (so they will like the pastor) can become the driving force for everything. But that is an impossible dream. As a lead pastor Andy encouraged his staff to keep in mind the mantra that, "everything we do upsets someone." And that is literally true. The thing that immensely pleases one individual or segment of the congregation can be regarded by others as the work of the devil. A leader will be criticized. That is a fact of life. But effective pastors discover that pursuing God's mission for the congregation is more important than keeping everyone happy. Edwin Friedman, in Failure of Nerve, observes that:

In any type of institution whatever, when (a leader) is being consistently frustrated and sabotaged…what will turn out to be true one hundred percent of the time is that the person at the top of that institution is a peace monger.[72]

---

[72] Edwin Friedman, A Failure of Nerve, New York, Seabury Books, 2007, 13.

4. For Laity, the essential shift is one of being transformed from Kingdom dwellers to Kingdom builders (or attending spectators to contributing disciples). In terms of the football field illustration, laity move from the stands onto the playing field of ministry. For many members, their church and the local country club have few differences – attend meetings, socialize, share meals, and have an occasional fundraiser. Kay Kotan, Director for the Center for Multiplying Disciples in the Arkansas Annual Conference of the United Methodist Church, has characterized the expectations of a church member as attending worship service, throwing a buck in the plate, and making sure the building is clean and maintained. While churches have extensive membership vows, the reality is closer to Kotan's criteria. As a result, there are a few people who truly serve God with their resources and they can become easily burned-out.

Kingdom builders are hampered, if not shut down, by pastoral micro-management and their need to be involved in everything. You cannot shift the culture of an organization through dictate, fancy statements, and special events. You shift the culture by empowerment, commitment (a compelling purpose & identity), and involvement (what one builds, one is committed to; in other words "ownership").

Christian faith is a journey; people serve as servants, not volunteers. People should be intentionally discipled, in Christian fundamentals and growing in Christ, before joining a committee or team. Contributing disciples meet Thom Ranier's six characteristics of church membership (adapted from his 2013 book I Am a Church Member[73]):

- I Will Be a Functioning Church Member
- I Will Be a Unifying Church Member
- I Will Not Let My Church Be about My Preferences and Desires

---

[73]Rainer, Thom S., *I am a Church Member*, B&H Publishing, Nashville, TN, 2013

- I Will Pray for My Church Leaders
- I Will Lead My Family to be Healthy Followers of Christ
- I Will Treasure Church Membership as a Gift, a Joyful Responsibility.

Kingdom builders also practice intentional discipleship – increasing in knowledge of God, intimacy with God, and serving others for God. Members shift from "going to church" to "being the church".

5. The FOCUS of the church must be a balance between member care and winning others to Christ by all – pastors and laity. As a church matures, it is easy to slip into an exclusive internal focus. This is in contrast to the planting of a church where the focus is weighted to the external, bringing people to church and ensuring that the surrounding community is aware that lives can be changed through involvement with the faith community.

Let's be clear: a congregation must provide care for existing members. In the rapid growth years at Glen Mar, Andy was confronted often with the perception that he cared more for the people "out there" than for the current members of the church. In the transformed church, it is essential that members receive care. It is not essential that they receive care directly from the pastor.

The wise spiritual leader will assure that adequate care is being provided. This is one area where clergy and laity partnering really pays off in increased mission and ministry. A "lone ranger" pastor can only care for so many individuals. A pastor operating primarily alone can only reach a limited number of those in need who are outside the congregation itself. Helping laity to identify their gifts and calling, subsequently deploying them in meaningful ministry, vastly expands the impact of the congregation. There are many ways this can happen: Stephen's Ministers, small groups vs. pastor-led studies, servants vs. volunteers (member expectations), etc.

An inward focus is often concerned with the scarcity of resources and wondering how things will get done. An outward focus trusts the promise that, when an individual or congregation is trying to do what God is calling them to do, God will provide whatever it takes for that calling to succeed.

The shifts in CHURCH and in FOCUS are closely related as seen in the chart below.

The Life Cycle of a Congregation

The key is to maintain a balance among renewed focus on Purpose (vision in the adjacent chart) & Identity, intentional discipleship development, and a joyful responsibility to serve others.

Do you have a specific strategy for reaching the unchurched?

CHURCH LIFE CYCLE

```
                    MATURITY
                  Adult
                  V R P M
     GROWTH    Youth         DECLINE
               V R P    Empty
               Child    Nest
                V R     R P M   Retire
         Infancy                P M
           V                         Old Age
                                        M
         BIRTH                        DEATH
```

V - Vision   R - Relationships   P - Programs   M - Management

Duty & Scraping By → **Finanaces** → **Generosity**

6. This shift from inward to outward focus almost always moves the congregation from operating with an attitude of scarcity to one of God's abundance. And this, of course, transforms how the church regards finances and giving. In the Financial Leadership Academy sponsored by the Mid Atlantic United Methodist Foundation (where Ted and Andy met while serving as leaders), a key concept was shifting the focus from budget and obligation to one of gratitude and generosity.

Many churches have developed a mindset of duty in terms of giving – which may work for the GI generation, but this works poorly for other generations. J. Clif Christopher describes the contrast well in his book *Rich Church, Poor Church – Keys to Effective Financial Ministry*.[74] Other non-profits emerge as options for church members and these non-profits speak about how they change lives. Meanwhile, the duty-bound church speaks of how much expenses have risen and how each member must raise their giving an equal percentage. Unfortunately, their backup plan is to go to half-time pastors, defer building maintenance, and consume endowment funds.

Churches should act more like philanthropic organizations in stewardship and fund raising. The focus of finances must be on the result produced by these resources and how lives are being changed. In other words, building a generosity mindset by emphasizing the outcome (value) of giving.

This is one of the key shifts in congregational culture, and one that produces huge benefits and effectively makes everything else easier. Creating a culture of generosity requires first doing the hard work of discerning purpose, identity, and context and working together as laity and clergy to change culture.

The Way We Always Did It → **Operations** → **Inspiring Practices**

7. This key shift moves the congregation from adherence to the "seven last words of the church" (We've always done it this way, or We've never done it this way), and toward an openness to risking new practices and procedures. Churches that choose to "play it safe" rarely experience gains in vitality. Fear of failure is a significant hindrance to growth in mission and ministry.

Typically, a lay person serves on a team/committee and they focus on how their predecessor did their job. The relationship of the job to God's commissions

---

[74]Christopher, J. Clif, Rich Church Poor Church: Keys to Financial Ministry, Abingdon Press, Nashville, TN, 2012

and their local church purpose and identity is not often understood. There are many inspiring practices that can be adapted (not adopted) by your church. An outward focus on how others do these tasks will make their execution more effective (closer to purpose & identity) and efficient (less time to achieve better results). Ultimately, the operation must be missional.

Relying on the way we've always done it implies a reliance on congregational ability alone and denies the awesome power of God to "do a new thing" in and through the congregation. Andy spent time at the U.S. Naval Academy (though God's call to ordained ministry led him to resign before graduating). He claims that one of the most important lessons learned as a midshipman was that he could frequently do more than he thought possible if willing to take a risk. And when the power comes from God, and not from within, the possibilities are magnified.

Other paradigm shifts that may be considered are:

Church centric ➡	**God centric**
Worship as an end to itself ➡	**Worship first, serve second**
Doing Church ➡	**Being the Church**
Many smaller ministries ➡	**Fewer impactful ministries**
Leading the Change ➡	**Being the Change**

What new thing is God calling you to do as an individual, that you might fulfill your God-given purpose? What new endeavor is God calling your congregation to undertake in order to reach more people with the Gospel, and with hope, healing and help? What would you do if you knew you couldn't fail? Our prayer is that this book has helped you to see new possibilities and given you the confidence needed to partner together as laity and pastors committed to courageous leadership in the uncharted waters of this chaotic and challenging world.

APPENDIX A

Benefits of Using a Coach

PRAYER

Gracious God, we are often inclined to think more highly of ourselves than we ought to think, assuming that we can "do it ourselves" without assistance from others or dependence on you. Help us to recognize and acknowledge our limitations. Prevent our pride from leading us to not ask for help when help is needed. Lead us to those persons who can guide us in our efforts to move our congregation closer to your will for us. We pray in Jesus' name. Amen.

SCRIPTURE

"You're going to find that there will be times when people will have no stomach for solid teaching, but will fill up on spiritual junk food—catchy opinions that tickle their fancy. They'll turn their backs on truth and chase mirages. But you—keep your eye on what you are doing; accept the hard times along with the good; keep the Message alive; do a thorough job as God's servant."

(The Message Version)

The Role of the Coach in Congregational Leadership
By Chris Holmes, PCC

Dawna Markova has written a powerful poem, "I will not die an unlived life." Most of us have a folder in our minds where we file our thoughts, our dreams, our wonderings, and our notions about what might be different or possible. Among the many folders in our minds, it stands out as the most colorful and exciting, its roots running deep into our heart and our soul. In that folder, God-sized possibilities bubble and churn. It is the seedbed for living the "fully lived life" of which the poet writes.

However, many of us live a different life—the one where we show up to work, answer the email, and start spinning the plates that we've always spun—because that is what we do. This life bobs along with what is put in front of us. Congregations and congregational leadership are all too familiar with this kind of life where time is spent doing what is safe, doing what we know how to do, and caring for the needs of the institution.

Intention empties the content of the colorful folder containing "God-sized possibilities" into the life a congregation could be living. Congregational teams sometimes get there on their own, but it is much easier with a conversation partner, a co-conspirator, a champion completely committed to the team's success. We call that conversation partner a coach.

A coach does no diagnosing as a counselor would, no fixing as a consultant would, and no molding as a mentor might. A coach gets curious, asks questions, stirs possibilities, and nudges toward commitment. A coach trusts that the congregational team, made up of the pastor and church leadership, holds the answers because they are the experts in their own congregational setting. A coach believes every congregation is amazingly capable and resourceful.

Here are five tangible ways a coach can help a congregation.

A coach helps congregational leadership in the process of self-discovery and determining God's direction for the church through asking good questions, encouraging exploration, and challenging old patterns.

A coach challenges leaders to envision multiple possibilities when leaders see only one option.

A coach ministers through support and encouragement by championing the leaders and believing in the great scope of the congregation's ability.

A coach stays action oriented with conversations that help the team clarify goals which are translated into specific commitments with associated time-lines.

A coach will ask for built-in team self-accountability as a way of strengthening the follow-through of what God intends.

There is a strong gravitational pull in congregational systems to keep doing what we have been doing. Congregations are the least accountable organizations in society, endlessly rehashing situation. A coach can be the disrupter who challenges that pattern by asking the hard questions around the purpose of the church and what matters most.

It takes courage for clergy and congregational leaders to open and engage that colorful folder that contains the promise of transformation, to do the difficult work of reshaping the way ahead with greater intention about where God is leading. That great and holy work can most expeditiously be done with the help of a coach.

Chris Holmes leads The Holmes Coaching Group, Inc. specializing in coaching church vestries, pastors and denominational leaders. He is a United Methodist Pastor, and author of The Art of Coaching Clergy.

CALL TO ACTION:
- Watch Podcast Episode 77 at The Lewis Center for Church Leadership **"'Coaching Leaders and Congregations to Reach their Full Potential' featuring Chris Holmes" then discuss with your leadership team how a coach could be helpful to your congregation.**
- Check with your judicatory to see if there is a list of trained and certified coaches available in your area.
- Recommend the use of a coach to your church council or administrative body.

APPENDIX B

ONE CHURCH'S TRANSFORMATION STORY
Growing as Disciples

Summary

Hockessin United Methodist Church (HUMC) underwent a change in leadership style and in culture. The key milestones for this transformation were:

1997-98	Vision for HUMC is created.
1999-2000	HUMC structure and roles are re-organized to meet the mission of the Church – to make disciples of Jesus Christ.
2001	HUMC Council begins spiritual development to become servant leaders
	Building plans for Christian education wing expansion approved.
2002	Third service (an informal, contemporary worship) and second Sunday School added.
	Choir director and organist resign; short, intense period of discontent.
2003	HUMC is blessed with many new members, growth in the contemporary service, addition of two new staff members and good financial strength.
	A new purpose statement is crafted and adopted.

Background

Hockessin United Methodist Church was founded in 1881 in a rural community ten miles northwest of Wilmington, DE. By the late 1990's, average worship attendance was 275 in two services. By 2006-2008, average worship attendance was 348 in three services.

Sunday School attendance in 2000-2001 was 114; it grew to 149 in 2003-2004.

Growing as Disciples

In January 1998 the traditional United Methodist structure of the Administrative Board and Council of Ministries were combined into the HUMC Council. The work of the Ad Board and the Council of Ministries was primarily information sharing and committee reports; most people saw them as duplicate meetings. Therefore, the structure change was made to reduce the duplication. This created a sixty-member Council, although attendance was usually twenty or below.

In November 1998 the HUMC Vision Team, under the leadership of Barbara Miller, completed its work and submitted its final report to the HUMC Council. The Vision Report generated little input or interest from the congregation as a whole. However, the steps1 toward making disciples of Jesus Christ became a key guide for later work.

In January 1999 the HUMC Council charters an Organizational Structure Review Committee to study the existing administrative and program structure and make organizational recommendations in order to recast the Church Council as servant leaders.

In July 1999 Bob Price replaces J.T. Seymour as Senior Pastor. After the Organizational Structure Review Committee interviews key church leaders and studies the vision report, the committee begins looking well beyond structure. It visits other churches in the area and studies other churches via books and the internet. The Purpose Driven Church by Rick Warren becomes the primary guide for the committee.

The committee makes its recommendation to the HUMC Council in April 2000. They describe their recommendations as transformational in terms of focus, roles, governance, congregational involvement and organization. The reasons for the change were leaders burning out, poor communication – including estrangement, fewer people willing to serve as leaders, a stifling structure that favored a glacial rate of change, and flat membership growth while the community grew 20% in the 1990s.

The essence of the Structure Committee's work shifted the Council focus from administrative to spiritual and servant leadership. The proposal included reduction of the Council size from 60 to 16 and the formation of ministry clusters[2] that bring common ministries together. The clusters were given unfamiliar names to signal the shift in emphasis. The change also included the covenant concept and written reports submitted well in advance of meetings in order to reduce the long meetings of endless reports. Meetings could focus on leadership/spiritual development and decision making.

The HUMC Council approved the Structure Committee recommendations in May 2000 and chartered a transformation committee. This committee met through the summer and chose "Growing as Disciples" as the transformational theme. Communications from the pulpit, through the church newsletter, and in open forums signaled the forthcoming change. The change was approved at the November 2000 charge conference and began with the 2001 calendar year. An abstract of the Council meeting began to appear in the monthly church newsletter.

Four sermons in September 2000 were devoted to the change that HUMC was about to undertake. Growing as Disciples and making disciples for Jesus Christ were common sermon themes through 2003. Toward the end of 2003 the sermons began to lay the groundwork for a living, vibrant personal covenant with God, beginning in 2004.

The HUMC Council changed its agenda to allot 20-30 minutes of each meeting to spiritual development – primarily using <u>The Purpose Driven Church</u>. The Council spent 2001 developing spiritually, learning to work in a different manner during Council meetings, and planning for physical expansion. In February 2001 the Council approved the master development plan and stage 1 – an expanded education wing.

The cluster of ministries concept started roughly in 2001 because few people felt called to be Cluster Leaders. Despite weekly appeals to the congregation for people to serve, few people step forward. Two of five positions are vacant most of the year. The Council reviewed the servant leadership and cluster concept in August 2001 and agreed to continue. Cluster updates were made in almost every monthly newsletter. As 2002 begins all five cluster leader positions are filled[7].

In March 2002 the concept of a third service, with a focus on contemporary worship and targeted at young families and seekers, was discussed. The concept was approved at the April Council meeting, pending details like Sunday School and parking. In June 2002 a letter is sent to the congregation about the third service and open forums are scheduled. The strong, urgent need for a Youth/Christian Education Director emerged during the open forums.

As a signal of change and importance, the Council met through the summer – normally a time of inactivity for HUMC leadership – to upgrade job descriptions and plan for the third service.

In September 2002 the new three service format begins with services at 8:30am, 9:45am and 11:00am. The order of worship and sermon delivery were traditional at the 8:30 and 11:00 services. The middle service features an informal atmosphere, praise singing and sermon delivery from the sanctuary floor. The essence of all three sermons is the same but the method of delivery differed. Standard Sunday School continues at 9:45am and Kid's Own Worship was conducted at the eleven o'clock hour.

In September 2002, a three-month period of discontent begins – catalyzed by the resignation of the Choir Director and the organist. The September-November Council meetings are standing room only as the congregation recognized that the Council was making changes. Some members claimed that there had been no communications and that a small group of people were making all the decisions. Others suggested that the building program be stopped – because of the poor economy since the 9/11/2001 World Trade Center disaster and discontent with the current HUMC leadership.

Another structure change was also approved – the formation of the Welcoming & Engaging New Disciples Cluster and the refocus of the Connecting Cluster into the Nurturing Cluster. This change was driven by the fact new people join the church and seem to disappear as rapidly. The challenge is large enough to devote a separate cluster to this important task.

The charge conference was held in December 2002 where disgruntled church members made their concerns and displeasures known to the District Superintendent. The disgruntled church members nominated no one to run against the people who were nominated to serve HUMC in leadership roles. John Mitchell acknowledged the efforts of the church leaders, encouraged all congregational members to get involved and express their perspectives, and to give SPRC input about pastor performance. The District Superintendent accepted the charge conference reports and supported the direction of HUMC. A handful of members stated that they will no longer attend HUMC.

In 2003 God blessed Hockessin United Methodist Church.

- In May the Council issues a new purpose for HUMC: To share the Love and Grace of Jesus Christ with Our Community[3].
- A Wednesday night fellowship dinner and study exceeds anyone's expectations with average attendance of seventy.
- New members join HUMC at a record rate for recent years.
- Financial solvency is better at year end than previous years.
- The date stone for the Building Expansion is laid in November 2003.

With the beginning of culture change in 2002, the following ensued.

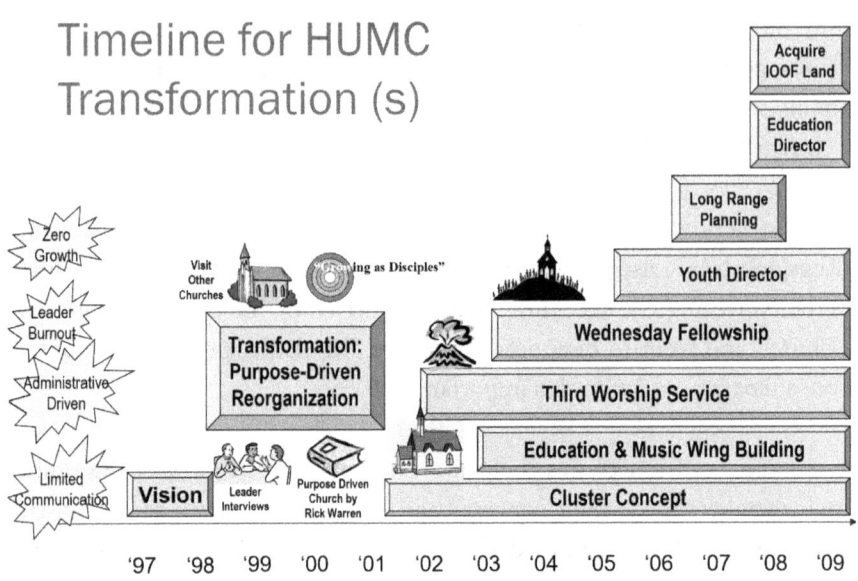

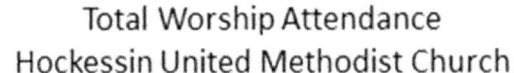

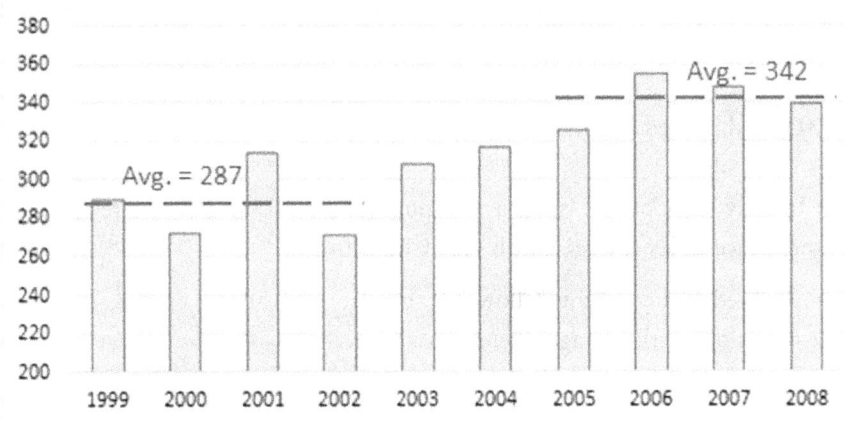

Church worship attendance rose.

[1] 1) Make Spiritual Growth Our First Priority, 2) Provide a Process for Member Care & Congregational Growth, 3) Establish a Small Group Ministry, 4) Recast Role of Church Council as Servant Leaders, 5) Develop Operating Covenants in All Ministry and Mission Groups, 6) Incorporate a Ministry of Money into Spiritual Growth of Each Individual, 7) Explore and Support New Ministries that Align with Desired Reality, and 8) Improve Facilities to Support Ministry and Mission Needs

[2] HUMC Ministry Clusters: Celebrating God as Disciples of Christ, Nurturing Disciples of Christ/ Fellowship (originally called Connecting Disciples of Christ), Developing Disciples of Christ, Reaching Out as Disciples of Christ, Communicating as Disciples of Christ and Welcoming & Engaging New Disciples (added January 2003)

[3] HUMC Purpose:
Share the Love and Grace of Jesus Christ with Our Community
To accomplish our purpose we:
- Welcome all people into our church family
- Celebrate and honor God through worship
- Serve our church, our community, and the world
- Grow spiritually through prayer and Bible study
- Nurture our congregation through small groups and Christian fellowship activities
- Share our faith and encourage others to become disciples of Jesus Christ
- Contribute to the support of our ministries according to the blessings God has given us

ACKNOWLEDGMENTS

We want to acknowledge our thanks for the following:

The Mid Atlantic United Methodist Foundation, especially Executive Director Jack Brooks and Assistant Director Annabelle Lusardi, for their undying encouragement and support.

Pastors and coaches of the several Financial Leadership Academies for helping us discern a unique message and focus our perspective.

Members of the churches we have served and with who we have consulted graciously endure our mistakes and learning with us how to achieve more vital ministries.

Our wives, Kay Brown and Joan Lunt, for their loving support and for putting up with our vacillating moods and erratic schedules as we worked on this book.

Megan Poling and the staff at Lucid Books for guiding two old guys through their first publishing venture.

And most importantly, we are grateful to God through the Holy Spirit for inspiring us with a vision and giving us the energy and enthusiasm to persevere.

To God be the glory!
Ted and Andy

ANDY LUNT

Since retiring in 2010, after 43 years in full-time ministry, Andy Lunt has served as Director of Vibrant Communities for the Baltimore Washington United Methodist Conference, working to start new faith communities and help existing congregations to grow and be revitalized, and as dean of the Financial Leadership Academy sponsored by the Mid Atlantic United Methodist Foundation. Andy has a Ph.D. in communications from the Univ. or MD and for 15 years, taught courses in preaching at Wesley Theological Seminary. He has been married for 57 years to Joan. They have two grown sons, two wonderful daughters-in-law, and two grandchildren.

TED BROWN

Ted is a retired executive from a large multi-national company, serving in executive management roles and consulting roles in strategy and improvement. He has been a coach/facilitator for twenty-five churches as part of the Mid-Atlantic United Methodist Foundation Financial Leadership Academy. He also helped two nonprofits in strategy development.

At Hockessin DE UMC, he held numerous leadership roles and led the culture change and reorganization of the church in 2001-03. In 2012, he started their small group ministry. He is a small group leader and men's retreat leader at his current church in middle Tennessee and serves on its Intentional Discipleship Team.

www.ingramcontent.com/pod-product-compliance
Lightning Source LLC
Chambersburg PA
CBHW060115170426
43198CB00010B/898